Kiplinger's

Estate
Planning

The Complete Guide to Wills, Trusts, and Maximizing Your Legacy

John Ventura, Esq.

KAPLAN PUBLISHING

New York

This publication is designed to provide accurate and authoritative information in regard to the subject matter covered. It is sold with the understanding that the publisher is not engaged in rendering legal, accounting, or other professional service. If legal advice or other expert assistance is required, the services of a competent professional should be sought.

Vice President and Publisher: Maureen McMahon
Editorial Director: Jennifer Farthing
Acquisitions Editor: Shannon Berning
Development Editor: Eric Titner
Production Editor: Fred Urfer
Production Designer: Datagrafix, Inc.
Cover Designer: Rod Hernandez

To Dean Richard Alderman of the University of Houston Law School,
a longtime consumer advocate and friend

Contents

What You Should Expect to Get Out of This Book

We spend most of our waking hours either working to earn money or thinking about what we'll do with our money—spending it, saving it, and investing it. Ironically, few of us give much more than a passing thought to what will happen to our money and everything we've bought with it when we die. In other words, most of us have done no estate planning. In fact, according to a Harris Interactive 2007 survey conducted for Lawyers.com and Martindale-Hubbell, an information resource for attorneys, 55 percent of all adult Americans don't even have a will. Wills are the estate planning documents that most people use to transfer their assets when they die. (You can find out more about the results of this study by going to *www.lexisnexis.com/about/releases/0966.asp* or *www.harrisinteractive.com/news/newsletters/clientnews/2007_lawyers.pdf*).

Other national studies have found that an even higher percentage of Americans have no estate plan whatsoever. That's bad news, because if you die without providing for the transfer of your assets using either a will or a living trust, the probate court in your area will determine who will inherit what you own according to

Estate planning is not just about who will get what you own when you die.

the inheritance laws of your state. In other words, your state will determine who gets your assets and that may not reflect your wishes. Furthermore, if you are in an unmarried relationship, the inheritance laws of most states won't give your partner a penny of what you own, no matter how many years you have been together.

Estate planning is not just about who will get what you own when you die. It's also about preserving the assets in your estate by having the appropriate insurance, minimizing the taxes your estate may owe when you die, and planning for the management of your finances and your medical care in case you become incapacitated and can't manage them for yourself. And it's about preparing a living will—a document that spells out the kinds of life-sustaining medical care you do and don't want if you are terminally ill or injured and close to death.

If you have young children, estate planning is also about using a will to legally designate the adult who will raise them and manage their assets if you and their other parent die before they become legal adults. If you don't make those designations, your state will decide who will play those critically important roles in your children's lives.

You may not relish the idea of estate planning. After all, it means adding one more responsibility to your already full plate, not to mention having to acknowledge the fact that someday you will die, an unpleasant reality that most of us would just as soon avoid. However, given all of the very important things that estate planning can accomplish, preparing a plan is the loving and responsible thing to do as a spouse, a partner, and as a parent.

I wrote *Kiplinger's Estate Planning* to provide you with an accessible, easy-to-understand introduction to estate planning, with the hope that it will motivate you to get your estate planning done. Given the complex maze of laws (probate law, state inheritance laws, tax laws, laws related to federal benefits like Medicaid, and laws related to death and dying), rules, and regulations associated with estate planning, I strongly recommend that you work with an experienced estate planning attorney. Even one seemingly small misstep or oversight can be very problematic, so working with someone who understands all of the legal and financial ins-and-outs of estate planning, and who can help you achieve all of your estate planning goals, is essential. Therefore, *Kiplinger's Estate Planning* provides you with all of the information you need to work effectively alongside an experienced estate planning professional.

Among other things, *Kiplinger's Estate Planning*:

- Will advise you on how to find a good estate planning attorney and about the services an attorney can provide.
- Features a helpful worksheet for inventorying all of your assets and debts, so you don't overlook anything when you are preparing your estate plan.
- Will help you define and achieve all of your estate planning goals.
- Highlights the unique estate planning issues faced by same-sex partners.
- Explains the importance and characteristics of a legally valid will, and what you can and can't accomplish with it.
- Guides you through the probate process—the process that all of the assets in your will must go through before they can be distributed to your beneficiaries.
- Tells you what a trust is, distinguishes between a testamentary trust (a trust that is created through your will after your death) and a living trust (a trust that you set up while you are alive), and provides detailed

information on using living trusts to accomplish your estate planning goals.

■ Offers straightforward explanations of the federal gift and estate taxes and the interrelationship between the two, and highlights strategies for reducing the amount of your estate that will go toward taxes when you die.

■ Educates you about using will substitutes, like life insurance, custodial accounts, retirement accounts, and inter vivos gifts—assets that you give away while you are alive.

Kiplinger's Estate Planning also includes information on estate planning for your spouse and your minor or adult children, and it includes issues you may want to take into account when you are planning for your family members. For example, if you are going to leave your children a large sum of money, it offers suggestions for how you can ensure that the assets you leave to them will have a positive effect on their lives. It also tells you about different trusts you can use to benefit your spouse when he or she is a poor money manager or has a serious disability.

In the book's final chapter, I explain why it's important to give someone you trust a durable power of attorney for your finances and a durable medical power of attorney. These people will manage your finances and your health care according to the instructions in your durable power of attorney documents if you become incapacitated. If you become incapacitated and do not have these documents, a probate court judge, in a public process, will choose the individuals who will make these decisions for you. I also explain the importance of preparing a living will. Without a living will, your loved ones will have to decide what to do—to make the excruciatingly difficult decision to "pull the plug," or keep you alive indefinitely and at great cost to your estate, using feeding tubes, respirators, and other medical interventions. When there is no living will, such life-and-death decisions rip many families apart.

Finally, *Kiplinger's Estate Planning* includes a detailed glossary of estate planning words and phrases using everyday language, not legalese.

If you would like additional information about the topics I cover in this book, check out *www.kiplinger.com*. It's loaded with useful estate planning information.

Estate planning can be challenging, but the information in *Kiplinger's Estate Planning* will help make the process less daunting. Congratulations on your willingness to do the hard work that will be so important to you and to your loved ones in the years to come!

The Hows and Whys of Estate Planning

Estate Planning Basics

Estate planning. It's essential! If you die without an estate plan, a probate judge will use the inheritance law of your state to determine who will inherit your hard-earned assets. The judge's decision may not reflect what you would have decided if you had taken the time to prepare a will or set up a living trust. A probate judge is a special kind of judge who presides over a state probate court. State probate courts mainly oversee the probating of wills, which includes ensuring that a will is legally valid and that a deceased person's property is distributed according to the terms of his or her will, among other things. Chapter 5 explains how the probate process works.

You may have the best of intentions about preparing an estate plan, but perhaps you always find "better" ways to spend your free time, and as a result, it doesn't get done. Maybe you never get around to it because an estate plan means acknowledging the cold, hard fact that someday you will die.

Some of you may not have an estate plan because you figure you're young and healthy, so you have all the time in the world to get your planning done. What's the rush? But let's be honest here, no one knows when his

Estate planning is a dynamic process that involves many different areas of the law, including property law, probate law, inheritance law, and tax law.

or her time will come. This is an especially important fact to keep in mind if you're the parent of minor children. Writing a will is the only legal means you have for designating the adult that will raise them if something should happen and you and their other parent both die. Is that really a decision you want a judge to make?

Some of you may not have done your estate planning because you assume that it's just for wealthy people like Donald Trump and Oprah, not for little old you. However, if you take time to add up the value of what you own right now—your home, savings, investments, your 401(k), your IRA, your car and boat, and so on—you may be surprised to discover how much you are worth. Besides, even if you don't have a bundle of money to leave behind when you die, there are plenty of other good reasons to have an estate plan.

Has your curiosity been piqued? Have you been convinced yet that you need a plan? If you still need persuading, the overview of estate planning in this chapter will clarify why it is so important and help you to see exactly what you can accomplish with your own estate plan. And for those of you who are reading this book because you already know that you need a plan, but you just can't seem to get it done, hopefully this chapter will convince you that there's no better time than the present to start your planning.

What Is Estate Planning and Why Is It Important?

Estate planning is a dynamic process that involves many different areas of the law, including property law, probate law, inheritance law, and tax law. Among other things, estate planning involves making decisions about:

- **Who will inherit your assets when you die.** Collectively, those assets are referred to as your *estate*, and the individuals and organizations you leave your property to are referred to as your *beneficiaries*.

- **How and when you will pass on your assets to your beneficiaries.** You can pass them on while you are alive, soon after your death, or sometime later. It all depends on what you want your estate plan to accomplish.

- **How to preserve the assets in your estate.** This will allow you to keep your assets available to you and your family while you are alive, and it will ensure that the maximum amount of those assets will be available to benefit your loved ones when you die.

- **How your assets will be managed if you can't manage them yourself because you're incapacitated as the result of an illness or injury.** Setting up guidelines for how your assets will be handled will ensure that your estate is properly managed.

- **How your health care will be managed if you are too ill or injured to make your own decisions.** During a time of serious illness or injury, the last thing you'd want for yourself or your family is for unresolved questions to arise regarding your health care.

- **How to minimize the amount of federal taxes your estate may owe when you die.** Assuming your estate is worth enough, without the appropriate planning, Uncle Sam will take a big share of what you own. How much is "enough" depends on the year in which you die, which is discussed in the next chapter. Some states impose their own tax on estates that are worth over a certain amount, but the federal tax takes the biggest bite. Reducing the federal tax burden is what estate planning attorneys focus on for clients with large

With the right planning, you too can minimize the potential tax liability on the assets that you leave to your surviving spouse and/or family members.

estates. With the right planning, you too can minimize the potential tax liability on the assets that you leave to your surviving spouse and/or family members.

The Benefits of Estate Planning

Estate planning is an act of love. It provides you with a legal means of taking care of those you hold closest to your heart after your incapacitation or death. It also helps you minimize the potential negative financial, legal, and emotional consequences for those you care most about. With the right planning, you can:

- Have your assets dispersed according to your wishes.
- Protect your beneficiaries.
- Ensure that your young children are raised with your best interests if they were to become orphans.
- Have your finances and health care properly managed if you become mentally or physically incompetent and can't manage your own affairs.
- Reduce the potential for disputes regarding your estate.
- Reduce the amount of federal and state estate taxes your estate may owe after your death.
- Create a personal legacy.

The Foundation of Your Estate Plan

Every estate plan is built on either a will or a revocable living trust. Which one should be the foundation of your estate plan depends, among other things, on the value and complexity of the assets in your estate, your family situation, how much control you want to exercise over the assets that you leave to your beneficiaries, and how much you want to spend on your estate plan (it costs more to set up a living trust than it does to write a will). Though most people make a will the foundation of their estate plans because wills are relatively quick and easy to prepare, living trusts have become increasingly popular in recent years, mainly because of their power and versatility. The following sections outline the main differences between a will and a living trust.

Wills

A *will* is a written document that spells out, among other things, to whom you are leaving your assets. Some wills also provide for the establishment of a trust upon the death of the will maker. This kind of trust is called a *testamentary trust*. For your will to be legally binding, it must comply with the requirements of your state.

When you die, all of the assets that you include in your will go through a process called *probate*. Probate is a state-supervised legal process that establishes the validity of a will and oversees the distribution of the deceased's estate according to the terms of the will. You'll learn more about this process in Chapter 5.

Living Trusts

A *living trust* is a kind of trust that is totally separate from your will. You set it up while you are still alive and competent. The assets that you transfer to a living trust become the property of the trust, so they won't go through the probate process when you die. This means that it costs less to distribute your assets through a living trust than it does through a will because your estate won't have to pay the costs of probate.

Having a living trust *does not* eliminate the need for a will. For example, you still need a will to:

If you're not sure whether you should build your estate plan on a will or a living trust, consult with an estate planning attorney.

- Designate a personal guardian for your minor children.
- Legally transfer to your beneficiaries the kinds of personal property that are not normally transferred to a living trust. Such property might include your knickknacks, books, bedding, kitchen equipment—anything that doesn't have a title, deed or other kind of legal ownership paperwork.
- Ensure that any property you may forget to transfer to your trust while you are alive gets transferred after your death. A will that transfers property to a living trust is called a *pour-over will.*

If you are relatively young and you don't have a lot of assets, it usually makes sense to build your estate plan on a will. However, as you acquire more assets, as they increase in value (hopefully), and as your family grows, you may decide to set up a living trust. If you're not sure whether you should build your estate plan on a will or a living trust, consult with an estate planning attorney.

Other Estate Planning Tools

A will and a living trust are not the only tools you can use to transfer your assets when you die. For example, you can own an asset with someone else as joint tenants. If you die first, your share of the asset will automatically transfer to your co-owner. Other available tools include the following items.

Life insurance. When you die, the insurance company that sold you the policy will pay a death benefit to whomever you've named as a beneficiary. Life insurance is a relatively inexpensive way to leave someone a substantial amount of money.

Retirement account. Examples of retirement accounts include individual retirement accounts, better known as IRAs, and employer-sponsored 401(k)s. Upon your death, the funds in these kinds of accounts will transfer to your designated beneficiary.

Investment account. Your investment account may hold mutual funds, individual stocks or bonds, and cash. When you die, all of those assets will go to your account beneficiary.

Payable-on-death account. A *payable-on-death (POD) account* is set up at a bank or at some other financial institution to hold assets on behalf of whomever you've designated as your account beneficiary. You can make your savings or checking account a POD account, and you can also hold a U.S. Savings Bond or a U.S. Treasury security in a POD account. Depending on your state, you may also be able to make your brokerage account a POD account.

Custodial account. You set up this kind of account to benefit a minor child, and you transfer the assets that you want the child to benefit from into the account, either while you are alive or after your death. When the child becomes a legal adult, or a few years later in some states, he or she will get control of whatever assets are in the account.

Inter vivos gift giving. An *inter vivos* gift is an asset that you give away while you are alive. You may give it to someone you know, a charity, your alma mater, or a living trust. Though there are other reasons to make inter vivos gifts, people with large estates often make them in order to decrease the value of their taxable estates.

If you hire an estate planning attorney to prepare your plan, the amount that you will spend depends on a number of different factors.

All of these estate plans are sometimes referred to as *will substitutes.* That's because they are a means of transferring the property that you own *outside* your will. In other words, they are not controlled by your will. You can learn more about will substitutes in Chapter 7.

Paying for Your Estate Plan

Many factors go into determining the cost of your estate plan. The first is whether you prepare your own plan or hire an estate planning attorney to prepare it for you. If you put your own plan together, the cost will be relatively small because you will probably prepare it by using estate planning software or by purchasing fill-in-the blanks forms, which are available at an office supply store for no more than $30, or at sites like LegacyWriter (*www.legacywriter.com*), 'Lectric Law (*www.lectlaw.com*), or U.S. Legal Forms (*www.uslegalforms.com*). Estate planning software like the latest version of Quicken WillMaker Plus should run between $30 and $80.

If you hire an estate planning attorney to prepare your plan, the amount that you will spend depends on a number of different factors. For example, most estate planning attorneys charge between $100 and $200 to prepare a simple will, one that does not include a testamentary trust, and about $500 if a will includes a trust. You should expect to pay an estate planning attorney somewhere between $1,000 and $5,000 to set up a living trust, depending on the complexity of the trust, such as whether it includes any subtrusts. The number of assets your attorney must transfer to the trust will also affect its cost.

The amount of money you spend on your estate plan, however, may pale in comparison to the costs associated with an insufficient plan or not having a plan at all. For example, if you will owe federal estate taxes when you die, the amount of your IRS tax liability could easily exceed by several times what it would cost you to hire an attorney. The estate planning attorney can prepare a plan that minimizes that debt and maximizes the amount of your estate that goes to your beneficiaries. Chapter 2 discusses estate taxes and explains how much your estate must be worth for you to owe these taxes.

Your estate plan should reflect your life, changing as your life changes.

Once You Have an Estate Plan

Don't do what most people do with their estate plans—they prepare one and then never look at it again. Your estate plan should reflect your life, changing as your life changes. Therefore, review your estate plan regularly—once a year is usually enough—to make sure that the wishes you've expressed in it have not changed and that your plan continues to accurately represent the state of your finances and the composition of your family. Here are some examples of when you should revise your plan.

- You add a child to your family.
- You get divorced or become a widow(er).
- You get married or remarried.
- You acquire new assets.
- You sell or lose assets.
- Your personal wealth increases, which may mean that you'll owe federal estate taxes when you die.

This chapter provided you with an introduction to some of the topics and issues of estate planning. For example, you found out why you need an estate plan and what you can accomplish with it. You also learned that you can build your plan on either a will or a living trust. The chapter also told you about other estate planning tools, including retirement assets, life insurance, joint tenancy ownership, and more, and provided brief explanations of how each tool works. The chapter explained why you should prepare a durable power of attorney for finances and the appropriate advance directives, and it discussed the cost of preparing an estate plan. You'll learn more about many of the basics of estate planning in the next chapter.

Getting Ready to Prepare Your Estate Plan

ow that you have an appreciation of why estate plans are so important, it's time to learn about some of the planning preliminaries you'll need to get out of the way, regardless of whether you prepare your own plan or an attorney does it for you. Those preliminaries include:

- **Defining your estate planning goals.** Your goals will help determine what your final plan looks like.
- **Understanding how your assets are titled.** In most states, the way your assets are titled determines what you can and can't give away through your estate plan.
- **Getting clear about your state's marital property law.** That law will also affect what you can and can't give away.
- **Understanding your business and how it fits into your estate plan.** If you own a business, it is essential to begin grappling immediately with all of the important and sometimes complex issues that are a part of estate planning, especially if your business represents a key portion of your estate's value.
- **Understanding how federal estate and gift taxes work.** If your estate is worth enough that you will owe

Goal setting is a critical first step because your goals will help shape your plan.

estate taxes when you die, it's important to put in place strategies for reducing the size of your taxable estate.

■ **Preparing a written inventory of your assets and your debts.** This list should be as complete and comprehensive as possible. The information is fundamental to creating your estate plan.

Figuring Out Your Estate Planning Goals

Goal setting is a critical first step because your goals will help shape your plan. For example, they will help determine whether or not you build your estate plan on a will or a living trust, whether you give some of your assets away while you are alive, and so on. To get you thinking, here are some examples of the kinds of goals you might want to establish for your estate plan.

■ **Make certain that your spouse and children will be taken care of financially after your death or incapacitation.** This is an especially important goal if you are your family's major breadwinner. Without the appropriate planning, your death or incapacitation could have devastating financial consequences for your family.

■ **Minimize the number of assets in your estate that will go through probate when you die.** All of the assets that are in your will go through the probate process, and the more assets there are, the more the process will cost your estate. Also, the assets in your will cannot be distributed to your beneficiaries until the probate process is over.

■ **Ensure that your assets will go to your current spouse when you die, and that a certain amount of those assets will go to your children after your spouse's**

death. This may be a very important goal for you if you are married for the second or third time, and your children are from your previous marriage(s). Without the appropriate planning, your current spouse may use up all of your assets after your death, give them away to his or her own children, or remarry and leave everything to the new spouse.

- **Keep the probate court out of the lives of your young children if you and their other parent both die while they are still young.** When you leave your assets to your children directly through your will, whomever you have designated as their property guardian will mange those assets while the children are minors. That person will have to comply with probate court–imposed rules, restrictions, and reporting requirements, and what your children have inherited from you and what their property guardian does with their assets will be part of the public record.

- **Provide for your disabled child without jeopardizing his or her eligibility for government assistance.** When you set up the right kind of trust, you can leave your disabled child (or a spouse, sibling, grandchild, and so on) a share of your estate without affecting his or her eligibility for important government benefits like Supplemental Security Income and Medicaid.

- **Fund your children's or your grandchildren's college educations.** You can leave money to your children or grandchildren in your will, set up an education trust for them, or establish and fund a 529 college plan for each child. This is a kind of educational savings program that is available in all states.

- **Benefit your favorite charity.** Giving to the causes you care about is a great way to reduce the size of your taxable estate because of the federal charitable deduction.

Appropriate estate planning can help you transfer your business before or after your death or incapacitation without compromising its integrity or value.

■ **Protect your business.** Appropriate estate planning can help you transfer your business before or after your death or incapacitation without compromising its integrity or value.

■ **Minimize the amount of federal estate taxes your estate will owe.** The less your estate owes in estate taxes, the more there will be to benefit your beneficiaries.

■ **Control the kinds of life-sustaining medical care and treatment you'll receive at the end of your life.** Without the right estate planning, your estate could be consumed by medical care and treatment you do not want.

If you work with an estate planning attorney, he or she will talk with you about your goals and the best ways to achieve them. The attorney may also suggest other goals you should consider in light of your finances and your family situation.

Individual and Joint Assets

The only assets you can give away through your estate plan are the assets that you own. They may include assets that you own 100 percent of—your individual assets—as well as your share of assets that you own with someone else—your joint assets. How the assets are titled, as well as the marital property law of your state—whether your state is a separate property or a community property state—determines what is and isn't yours to give away. You can find out about these subjects by talking to an estate planning attorney or by searching the Internet.

Many of your assets may be titled as joint assets. This means that you own them with someone else. They may be titled as *joint tenancy with the right of survivorship* assets, *tenancy by the entirety* assets, or *tenancy in common* assets.

Joint Tenancy with the Right of Survivorship Assets

When an asset is titled like this, you and your co-owner(s) each own an equal share of the asset. When one co-owner dies, his or her share is divided equally among the remaining co-owners. For example, if you and your spouse own an asset as joint tenants (married couples usually own their homes and bank accounts as joint tenants) and you die first, your half of the asset automatically goes to your spouse. Therefore, you can't transfer your share of a joint tenancy asset through your estate plan, because when you die, your share is automatically transferred by virtue of the way it's titled.

Tenancy by the Entirety Assets

This kind of joint ownership works like joint tenancy ownership. Therefore, you can't control who will end up with your share of an asset that's titled this way. This form of ownership is only available to spouses in some states.

Tenancy in Common Assets

If you own an asset with at least one other person as *tenants in common*, each of you is legally entitled to leave your share of the asset to whomever you want in your estate plan.

Separate Property and Community Property States

If you are married, the marital property law in your state determines what you and your spouse own together and separately, and therefore affects what you can and can't give away through your estate plan. Most states are separate property states, also known as common law states.

However, nine states are community property states: Arizona, California, Idaho, Louisiana, Nevada, New Mexico, Texas, Washington, and Wisconsin.

Separate Property States

If you live in a separate property state, with a few exceptions, the money that you earn during your marriage is 100 percent yours, and the assets that you buy with that money also belong only to you. A possible exception would be if you put your spouse's name on the ownership paperwork for an asset that you own—the title to your car or the deed to your rental property, for example—as a joint tenant with the right of survivorship or as a tenant by the entirety. Also, any assets that you and your spouse may purchase together during your marriage are legally owned only by you if your name is on the title—even if your spouse helped pay for them. Therefore, when you are preparing your estate plan in a separate property state, you can give away all of the money you've accumulated in your own name and all of the assets that you've purchased before and during your marriage. You can also give away all of the assets that are in your name only, whether you acquired them before or during your marriage, through your estate plan.

Community Property States

Things work quite differently in community property states. In these states, spouses each have an automatic 50 percent ownership interest in all of their marital assets—all of the income either of them earns during their marriage and all of the assets that either or both of them acquire while they are married, regardless of who pays for the assets and whose name is on the ownership paperwork. In other words, in these states, marital property law trumps the way assets are titled when it comes to what you can and can't give away in your estate plan.

Therefore, if you live in a community property state, you can use your estate plan to give away only your one-half interest in your marital assets. However, with a few exceptions, you can also give away any money that you earned and any assets that you acquired prior to your marriage, as well as any assets someone may have given to you or that you may have inherited during your marriage. Those exceptions include if you give your spouse a legal share of one of your separate assets or if you unintentionally convert some of your separate property into community property. You can do this by spending money that belongs to you and your spouse on an asset that belongs just to you. For example, you take money out of the bank account that you share with your spouse to remodel rental property that you purchased when you were single. When you do this, you are said to be *commingling your community property with your separate property.*

The way your business is structured affects your estate planning options.

Your Business and Your Estate Plan

If you own your own business or have an interest in a business, it may represent a substantial portion of your estate's total value, and it may be an essential source of income for you and your family. Therefore, as indicated in the previous discussion of estate planning goals, it's important to take into account your business's legal structure and the implication of that structure for your estate plan.

Types of Businesses

The way your business is structured affects your estate planning options. Therefore, you may want to discuss with an estate planning attorney whether it would be wise to change your business's legal structure while you are alive and mentally competent. By doing so, it may be easier to transfer ownership of your business and to reduce your future estate tax liability. The following are some of the most common types of business structures.

Sole proprietorship. If you run your business as a sole proprietorship, you own 100 percent of it. Your business assets are treated as your personal assets, and you are personally responsible for all of your business's debts and other liabilities.

Partnership. When you run your business as a partnership, you own it with at least one other person. You and your partners are personally responsible for each other's partnership debts and other liabilities.

Corporation. A business that is structured as a corporation is a legal entity that exists separate and apart from its owners, unlike sole proprietorships and partnerships. The business is shielded from the impact of any personal financial or legal problems you and your co-owners may have, although there are exceptions. Most family-owned businesses are incorporated.

Limited liability corporation (LLC). An LLC is similar to a corporation, but with some differences. It's like a corporation because an LLC is its own legal entity, and LLC owners are not personally liable for their business's debts and other liabilities. However, a LLC is not taxed like a corporation. Instead, LLC owners report the profits or losses of their business on their personal income tax returns, so they avoid the problem of double taxation that's associated with corporations.

Limited partnership. This business structure combines features of a partnership with features of a corporation. It is commonly used to own and manage real estate and other kinds of business investments. Every limited partnership has at least one general partner. The general partner runs the business day to day and is personally liable for its debts and other obligations. The limited partner also owns a share of the business (but less than a general partner) and has limited personal liability for the business.

Issues to Consider

To get you thinking, here is a sampling of the kinds of estate planning–related issues you'll need to make decisions about as a business owner, although some of the issues may not be relevant, depending on how your business is structured.

How long do I intend to be involved in my business?

Do you intend to maintain your current level of involvement and investment for the foreseeable future, or do you want to begin phasing yourself out of the business gradually? If you want to phase yourself out, what's the best way for that to happen?

After I die, what do I want to happen to my business?

Do you want it to continue operating and providing income for your family; do you want it to be sold? Should it be shut down, and should its assets be liquidated? Given what you want, what should you be doing now to prepare?

If I want my business to continue generating income for my family, who is going to own it and manage it?

If the business is a family business, do you have a sensible succession plan? A succession plan spells out who will run your business when you can't or don't want to run it anymore, and exactly how that transition will happen.

You should have insurance to protect your business and your family, as well as to preserve the value of your estate.

What will happen to my business if I become temporarily or permanently incapacitated? You can provide for the ongoing management of your business under such circumstances by making certain that the person you appoint as your financial agent has the know-how to run your business, at least for a brief time, and/or the authority to transfer it to a trust, among other powers.

How much is my business (or my share of the business) worth? What are your options for transferring ownership of the business? Depending on how your business is structured, your options may include selling the business to one or more people while you are alive, gifting shares of your business over a period of years while you are alive, and preparing a buy-sell agreement.

What are the tax implications if I sell my business or give it away over time? It's important to understand how selling off your business over time will affect the value of your estate, the amount of taxes your estate will owe when you die, and the amount of estates taxes your surviving spouse (or partner) might owe.

What implication does the legal structure of my business have for my estate plan? Should I change that structure? In the "Types of Businesses" section of this chapter, the most common kinds of business legal structures are reviewed and some of the estate planning issues associated with each one are highlighted. Don't change your business's legal structure for estate planning purposes without consulting with an attorney.

Do I have the right kinds of insurance? You should have insurance to protect your business and your family, as well as to preserve the value of your estate.

If I still own my business when I die, how will it affect the amount of federal estate taxes my estate may owe? If you die without having taken this issue into account through your estate planning, your family may be forced to sell your business to pay your estate tax debt. As a result, they may lose the very asset you expected would provide them with a steady stream of income after your death.

Do I want my business to go through probate? Probably not, considering that the cumbersome nature of the probate process may make it difficult for your business to be managed in a sound and timely manner, which could have a negative effect on your business's value and ongoing viability.

Understanding How Federal Estate and Gift Taxes Work

The federal estate tax and the federal gift tax are part of a complex, interrelated tax system that can be confusing. Though the ins and out of these two taxes and how to minimize the amount of taxes your estate may owe when you die are probably best left to an estate planning attorney, you should at least have a passing familiarity with how each tax works if the value of your estate is substantial. Therefore, this section provides you with just enough information to get your feet wet.

Federal Estate Taxes

When you die, if your taxable estate is worth more than the amount of your federal lifetime tax exclusion, your estate will have to pay federal *estate taxes* (also known as *inheritance* or *death taxes*) on the excess before all of your assets can be distributed to your beneficiaries.

Currently, the maximum federal tax rate is 45 percent, but that could change if Congress amends the law, which many estate planning experts expect will happen. Figure 2.1 lists the amounts of the federal tax exclusion, depending on the year in which you die, according to the federal Economic Growth and Tax Relief Reconciliation Act (EGTRR), which is the current law (Congress passed it in 2001).

Figure 2.1

Federal Estate and Gift Taxes

This chart illustrates the amount of the lifetime federal estate exclusion by year from 2008 to 2011 as well as the maximum tax rate for estates that are worth more than the exclusion amount. It also shows the size of the gift tax credit that you are entitled to each year and the amount of your federal gift tax exclusion.

Federal Estate Tax			Federal Gift Tax	
Year of Death	**Lifetime Estate Tax Exemption**	**Federal Estate Tax Rate**	**Applicable Credit**	**Applicable Exclusion**
2008	$2 million	45%	$345,800	$1 million
2009	$3.5 million	45%	$345,800	$1 million
2010	Federal estate tax repealed	N/A	$345,800	$1 million
2011	$1 million	55%	$345,800	$1 million

When you look at this information, bear in mind that in 2009, with a new administration in Washington, it's anticipated that Congress will increase the exemption amount for 2011 and going forward from $1 million to around $3.5 million. However, no one knows for sure whether the law will be changed and exactly how it will be changed, making estate tax minimization planning quite a challenge. Given this uncertainty, if you have a substantial estate and are concerned about federal estate taxes, it would be best to stay up-to-date regarding what Congress decides to do and to be ready to revise your plan accordingly.

The amount of estate taxes your estate will owe is determined by the following.

Fair market value is the amount that your assets are worth at the time that you die, not what you paid for them.

Your estate's gross fair market value at the time of your death minus any expenses and deductions to which you may be entitled. The current gross *fair market value* of your estate represents all of the assets that you own and control when you die. Fair market value is the amount that your assets are worth at the time that you die, *not* what you paid for them. For tax purposes, those assets include:

- Your share of any jointly owned assets.
- Your retirement accounts, including IRAs, 401(k)s, and so on.
- Certain types of annuities that are payable to your estate or to a beneficiary.
- All life insurance proceeds that are payable to your estate or to your policy beneficiaries if the policy is in your name.
- Other assets with a beneficiary designation, including assets in a payable-on-death account.
- Any life insurance policies that you may have transferred to someone else within three years of your death.
- All real estate that you own at the time of your death.
- Your bank accounts.

Presently, because of the EGTRR, when you die directly affects the amount of federal estate taxes your estate may owe.

■ Living trust assets that you controlled and/or benefited from while you were alive, but not assets that you've transferred to an irrevocable living trust.
■ Your business assets.
■ Assets that you gave away within three years of your death, under certain circumstances.

Expenses include the costs of probating your estate, your funeral expenses, any claims against your estate such as unpaid debts, and any other outstanding obligations you may have at the time of your death.

Allowable deductions include the *marital deduction* and the *charitable deduction*, among others. These and other deductions are discussed later in this section.

The year that you die. Presently, because of the EGTRR, when you die directly affects the amount of federal estate taxes your estate may owe. As Figure 2.1 illustrates, for example, under that law, if you die in 2009 you can exempt $3.5 million worth of your taxable estate from the estate tax. In other words, you can pass on up to $3.5 million worth of your assets tax-free, but your estate will have to pay taxes on any portion of your estate that exceeds that amount. That $3.5 million is referred to as your *lifetime federal estate tax exemption.* But if you die in 2010, the federal estate tax goes away (but just for that year), which means that no matter what your estate is worth, it won't owe a dime in estate taxes to the federal government. Under current law, the estate tax returns in 2011, and the federal exemption is reduced from $3.5 million to $1 million for that year and future years. However, as previously mentioned in this chapter, Congress is expected to amend the law and increase the exemption amount for 2011 and beyond to somewhere around $3.5 million.

If the value of your estate is substantial, tax minimization planning will be a challenge for you because of these changes and because of the uncertainty regarding exactly what will happen to the amount of the estate tax exemption starting in 2011. Therefore, you can expect your planning to be constantly in flux for the next few years.

The amount of any taxable transfers you may have made while you were alive. While you are alive, you can give your property away to reduce the size of your taxable estate so that your estate will owe less in taxes when you die. However, there are federal limits on how much you can give away each year to any one person, and also on the total amount you can give away during your lifetime. If you give away more than the federal limits, the excess amount will affect your total tax liability when you die. "The Federal Gift Tax and How It Relates to the Federal Estate Tax" part of this chapter explains these federal limits and how the gift tax works, including the federal limits on annual gift giving.

The amount of any deductions. The "Some Gifts Aren't Subject to Taxation" section of this chapter explains these deductions.

State Estate Taxes

Your state may assess its own estate tax. If it does, however, its tax won't take nearly as big a bite out of your estate as the federal tax will. Therefore, estate tax minimization focuses on the federal tax. Also, the amount of taxes that your estate pays to your state will be deducted from the total amount that you owe to the IRS.

The federal gift tax is a tax on assets that you give away while you are alive—inter vivos gifts.

The Federal Gift Tax and How It Relates to the Federal Estate Tax

As explained at the start of this discussion about taxes and your estate, and as Figure 2.1 helps to illustrate, the federal estate and gift taxes are interrelated. The federal gift tax is a tax on assets that you give away while you are alive—inter vivos gifts. It exists to ensure that you don't give away everything that you own while you are still living in order to avoid owing any federal estate taxes when you die. Uncle Sam always stays one step ahead of you!

Here is how the gift tax works: Every calendar year, you can give up to $12,000 worth of inter vivos gifts to as many people as you want. If you are married, you and you spouse can coordinate your gift giving and together, you can give a total of up to $24,000 to whomever you want, tax-free, every calendar year. The $12,000 is referred to as your *annual gift tax exclusion* or *annual exclusion.* However, the amount of this exclusion is automatically adjusted for inflation in increments of $1,000. For example, it's expected to increase to $13,000 in 2009.

If you give someone more than $12,000 worth of assets in a given calendar year, you must file a gift tax return with the IRS on the excess amount—the difference between the total amount that you gave to that person and your $12,000 per person annual gift tax exclusion. You won't have to pay the tax at that point however. Instead, the amount will be credited against—subtracted from—your $1 million lifetime gift tax exclusion, dollar for dollar (see Figure 2.1). If you use up the total amount of that exclusion while you are alive, then when you die your estate will owe a *gift tax* on the amount that exceeds the exclusion. The tax rate mirrors the federal estate tax rate.

This exclusion can be described in two ways. It is the amount of assets that you can transfer without your estate having to pay any estate taxes when you die, which represents your $2 million lifetime estate tax exclusion, assuming that you die in 2008—or your $3.5 million lifetime estate tax exclusion if you die in 2009. Or the exclusion is a tax credit of $345,800, which equals the amount of taxes your estate would have to pay on those assets if there was no $1 million gift tax exclusion.

Strategies for Reducing the Size of Your Taxable Estate

While you are alive, you can take actions to minimize—maybe even entirely eliminate—the amount of taxes you may owe when you die. These actions include the following.

Spend every penny you've got. If there is no one in your life that you want to take care of through your estate plan, or if you feel no obligation to leave anyone anything, then live it up! Enjoy the fruits of your labors while you are alive. However, make sure that you plan for the possibility that toward the end of your life you may need expensive medical care, need to be put in a nursing home, or may require expensive in-home care.

Remove assets from your taxable estate through inter vivos gift giving. Whenever possible, give away assets that you expect will appreciate in the coming years—real estate and stocks, for example. That way, those assets will appreciate in someone else's estate, not in yours. To be treated as inter vivos gifts, the assets that you give away must meet some very specific criteria. Otherwise, your gifts will not help reduce the size of your taxable estate. The following is a summary of the very specific IRS criteria your gifts must meet to benefit your estate.

> While you are alive, you can take actions to minimize—maybe even entirely eliminate—the amount of taxes you may owe when you die.

■ **The beneficiary of your gift must benefit from it now, not later.** For example, if you give some of your rental property to your adult daughter, the IRS will not treat your gift as an inter vivos gift unless you have actually transferred title to that property out of your name and into hers.

■ **You can't continue to benefit from the asset you've given away.** Using the rental property as an example, if you continue receiving income from the property once your daughter owns it, then in the eyes of the IRS you have not made an inter vivos gift.

■ **You cannot continue to control the asset in any way after you've given it to someone, nor can you take it back.** Returning to the example of the rental property, if you are deciding how much rent to charge, collecting the rents, and so on, then you have not made an inter vivos gift.

Transfer your assets to an irrevocable trust. *Irrevocable trusts,* which include a life insurance trust, a *charitable remainder trust,* and a *charitable lead trust,* provide you with a means of getting assets out of your estate while you are alive. These are covered in more detail in Chapter 6.

Transfer your business interest. If you have a family business, your interest in that enterprise may represent a large portion of your estate. However, you can get that asset out of your estate by transferring it over time to your family members, who will probably be your children, through a family limited partnership or a family limited liability company.

Some Gifts Aren't Subject to Taxation

In addition to your right to give away up to $12,000 tax-free every year to as many people as you want, while you are alive you can make other kinds of gifts, no matter how large, that won't have any affect on the amount of taxes you will owe. These other kinds of gifts are referred to as *federal estate tax deductions*. They include:

- **Unlimited marital tax deduction.** Assuming your spouse is an American citizen, you can give him or her as much of your estate as you want while you are alive with no impact on your federal estate tax liability. You can also transfer to your spouse as many assets as you want, which will be estate tax–free when you die, regardless of their value.

- **Charitable deduction.** You can transfer an unlimited amount of your assets while you are alive, or after your death, to as many IRS-approved charities as you want. To find out if a particular charity is IRS-approved, go to *apps.irs.gov/app/pub78*. The IRS updates this list regularly.

- **Educational deduction.** You can pay for someone else's tuition, but you must write your check to the educational institution itself, not to the student who will benefit. For example, you can pay your grandchild's annual $40,000 college tuition by writing a check to his or her college. And in addition, each year you can give your grandchild up to $12,000 in inter vivos gifts—maybe to help defray the cost of his or her room and board at college, for books and supplies, and so on. You can also contribute up to $60,000 in a single year (which is equivalent to five years' worth of $12,000 gifts) to a 529 plan. This contribution will not reduce the amount of your lifetime federal estate tax exclusion, as long as you don't contribute any more money to the plan over the next five years. However, if you die before the five years are up, a portion of your contribution *will* be included in your taxable estate.

- **Medical deduction.** You can pay an unlimited amount of someone else's medical expenses, including the

Creating a written inventory of everything that you own and owe is an essential estate planning preliminary.

cost of his or her medical insurance and/or long-term care insurance, if you write your check directly to the medical provider.

■ **Political deduction.** If you live and breathe politics, you can make an unlimited amount of tax-free gifts to the political organizations you support.

Inventorying Your Assets (and Your Debts, Too)

Creating a written inventory of everything that you own and owe is an essential estate planning preliminary. This inventory will:

■ Help you make certain that you don't overlook any of the assets that you own (in whole or in part) when you're preparing your plan. If you do, a probate judge will distribute them according to your state's inheritance law, not according to your wishes, after your death.

■ Make it easier for you to think about who you want to leave each of your assets to, because everything that you own will be recorded in one place.

■ Help you calculate the approximate total value of your estate so you will know whether you need to be concerned about the amount of federal estate taxes your estate may owe when you die. That number will be determined by adding up the total value of all of the assets in your probate estate and subtracting from that all of your probate expenses, debts, and any deductions you may be entitled to take. For the purposes of this inventory, all you need to do is compare the total current value of all of your assets to the amount of debt that you owe. If you end up with a number that is well below the amount of your federal unlimited estate tax exemption (see Figure 2.1 for that amount), then you don't need to worry about estate tax minimization for now. However, that may change over time as you acquire additional assets, if your current assets appreciate in value, if you receive an inheritance, and/or as you pay down your debts. Also, once you begin working with an estate planning attorney, he or she will evaluate your finances to get a more accurate fix on whether you will be liable for estate taxes. If you will be, your attorney will help you implement an effective tax minimization plan. All of the factors that your attorney will take into account are explained in this chapter.

It's important to update your inventory periodically because the assets in your estate, as well as the value of your estate, will change over time.

It's important to update your inventory periodically because the assets in your estate, as well as the value of your estate, will change over time. For example, you may need to add or subtract assets, increase or decrease the value of the assets on your inventory form, add debts, remove debts as you pay them off, and so on. Whenever you revise your inventory information, take time to figure out whether the changes you've made have affected the amount of federal estate taxes you may owe.

Determining Your Assets

To complete the following estate planning inventory forms, you must categorize your assets as either *real property* or *personal property*. Real property is the real estate you may own, including your home or condo, vacation home, rental property, undeveloped land, your interest in a time-share, and so on. Locate all of the ownership paperwork for each piece of real property that you own so that you can identify how each asset is titled.

The rest of your assets fall into the personal property category. They may include your bank accounts,

An asset's current market value is what it's worth today— what you would have to pay for the asset if you bought it today— not what you originally paid for it.

certificates of deposit (CDs), stocks, mutual funds, bonds, annuities, life insurance policies, retirement accounts, cars, motorcycles, boats, RVs, jewelry, fine art, other collectibles like antiques and stamp and coin collections, as well as your business interests. Your personal property also includes miscellaneous items of lesser value like your clothing, furniture, cookware, knickknacks, photo albums, books, bedding and quilts, DVDs, gardening tools, and so on.

When working on the asset sections of your inventory forms indicate a current market value for each asset. An asset's current market value is what it's worth today—what you would have to pay for the asset if you bought it today—not what you originally paid for it. If you aren't sure what some of your assets are worth, talk with your stockbroker, financial planner, CPA, real estate agent, or life insurance agent, depending on the nature of the asset. If you own antiques, coin and stamp collections, fine art, fine jewelry, and business interests, you may need to hire an appraiser who specializes in valuing these particular kinds of assets.

Figure 2.2

What You Own: Real Property					
Asset Type and Location	Mortgage Holder	How You Own It	Percentage Owned	Amount Paid	Current Market Value
Total current value $					

Figure 2.3

What You Own: Personal Property (Liquid Assets)				
Type	Location of Asset	How You Own It	Percentage Owned	Current Market Value
Checking Accounts				
Total current value $				
Savings Accounts				
Total current value $				
Money Market Accounts				
Total current value $				
Income From a Trust				
Total current value $				
Certificates of Deposit				
Total current value $				

Figure 2.4

What You Own: Personal Property (Stocks, Mutual Funds, Bonds, Etc.)					
Type	Account Number	Financial Institution	How You Own It	Purchase Price	Current Value
Stocks					
Total current value $					
Mutual Funds					
Total current value $					
Bonds					
Total current value $					

Figure 2.5

What You Own: Personal Property (Life Insurance Policies)				
Insurance Company	Policy Number	Death Benefit Amount	Beneficiary	Current Cash Value
Total current value $				

Figure 2.6

What You Own: Personal Property (Retirement Accounts)			
Type	Name of Institution	Account Number	Beneficiary Value
Total current value $			

Figure 2.7

What You Own: Personal Property (Stock Options)		
Type	Vesting Date	Current Value
Total current value $		

Figure 2.8

What You Own: Personal Property (Other Personal Assets)	
Type	**Current Value**
Cars	
Total current value $	
Boats	
Total current value $	
Other Watercraft	
Total current value $	
Motorcycles	
Total current value $	
Recreational Vehicles and Trailers	
Total current value $	
Fine Jewelry	
Total current value $	
Fine Art	
Total current value $	

What You Own: Personal Property (Other Personal Assets)	
Type	**Current Value**
Collectibles	
Total current value $	
Antiques	
Total current value $	
Furniture	
Total current value $	
Fine China and Silver	
Total current value $	
Furs	
Total current value $	
Money Owed	
Total current value $	
Other	
Total current value $	

Figure 2.9

What You Own: Personal Property (Business Interests)			
Type of Business	Legal Structure	Percentage of Ownership	Current Value of Your Interest
Total current value $			

Figure 2.10

What You Own: Personal Property (Royalties, Trademarks, Patents, Copyrights)		
Type	Percentage of Ownership	Current Value of Your Interest
Total Current Value $		

Figure 2.11

What You Own: Personal Property (Other Significant Assets)		
Type	Percentage of Ownership	Current Value of Your Interest
Total Current Value $		

Determining Your Debts

When you are filling out the debt section of the form in Figure 2.2, you will only need to list the debts that you signed for on your own, or that you and your spouse both signed for if you live in a separate property state. If you live in a community property state, you must list the outstanding debts that you as well as your spouse have incurred during your marriage. That's because each of you is 100 percent legally liable for each of them.

Figure 2.12

What You Owe		
Name of Creditor	**Amount of Debt**	**Portion of Debt For Which You Are Responsible**
Total Amount of Debt $		

To calculate the net approximate value of your estate, use the following formula:

Total Approximate Value of Your Assets
– Total Debts
―――――――――――――――――――――
= Total Approximate Value
  of Your Estate: $_____

What to Do About the "Small Stuff"

When you're filling out the asset sections of your inventory forms, you may wonder what to do about items such as your photo albums, cookbooks, quilts, kitchenware, knickknacks, clothing, gardening tools, cookie jar, and so on. Not only are most of those assets probably not worth very much, but listing and valuing each of them could take forever! However, don't ignore those assets! Some of your family members may have strong sentimental attachments to some of them. In fact, it's not at all unusual for individuals to fight over who will end up with the "small stuff" when someone dies and has left no instructions for who the assets should go to. Therefore, it's a good idea to decide whether you will give away such assets while you are alive or whether you want to establish a process for distributing them to your loved ones after your death.

First, find out if any of your children or grandchildren (or anyone else you are especially close to) has a special attachment to any of your miscellaneous items. Don't assume that you know. Avoid hurt feelings by making it clear that identifying something as being important to them is no guarantee that they will end up with it, especially if others want it too. In the end, it's your decision. Also, make certain that you have not already promised something to someone, and check with your spouse or partner to make sure that he or she didn't do the same.

Once you have a good understanding of who wants what, you can give those items away while you are still alive, or you can include them in your will. You may want to talk with your spouse or partner about what to do if you die first, so your spouse or partner can carry out your wishes if you did not express them in your will.

The following describes your options for any items that you are not leaving to specific persons in your will or giving away while you are alive.

Group Like Items Together in Your Will

Like items may include all of your bedding and towels, all of your cookware, all of your gardening tools and equipment, your sewing machine and all of your sewing supplies, and so on. In your will, you can leave each group of items to a specific beneficiary or to a group of beneficiaries. For example, "I leave all of my kitchen cookware, dishes, and glassware to my three adult children to be divided equally among them." Another option is to lump your miscellaneous items together as your "household effects," and then leave them to a specific beneficiary or group of beneficiaries. However, if you have already promised someone one of the items you would consider to be part of your household effects, then be sure to specify that in your will. For example, your will might say, "I leave all of my household effects to my three adult children, except for my mother's cookie jar. I leave that item to my oldest daughter, Sarah Farmington."

Stipulate How Your Family Members Should Divide Up Your Personal Belongings after Your Death

You can spell out in your will how you want your family to divvy up your miscellaneous assets once you are deceased. For example, you may instruct them to take turns choosing items after drawing straws or flipping a coin to determine who will choose first. You can also leave instructions that any items no one wants should be donated to a particular charity.

Tag or Label Items

You can put tags or labels on the back or the bottom of larger items, like furniture, rugs, lamps, artwork, decorative boxes, computers and computer equipment, and so on. The tag or label should indicate the name of the person who you want to have that particular item. You may also want to write a note that explains the significance of the item or why you are giving it to that particular person, and attach the note to the tag or label.

This chapter filled you in on the various kinds of information you should pull together and understand before you be down to the business of actually preparing your estate plan. It should now be obvious that you need to be clear about how your assets are titled and about whether you live in a separate property or community property state, because that information determines what is and isn't yours to give away through your estate plan. In addition, you should now be able to create a written inventory of your assets and debts. And you should be fully aware why it's important to decide what to do about the small, miscellaneous items that you own and to establish a specific process for distributing them to your loved ones, either while you are still alive or after your death. Finally, the importance of establishing specific goals for your estate plan should be clear, and the examples provided in this chapter should get you on the right path toward determining what your goals may be.

How an Estate Planning Attorney Can Help You

Chapter 3

If you're like a lot of people, when you think about preparing your estate plan, you tell yourself "I can do it myself." Perhaps you may not want an attorney's help because you're frugal and try to avoid spending money on professional help whenever possible. You may figure that you can create a perfectly adequate plan using estate planning software or some fill-in-the-blank forms. And you may be right. However, do-it-yourself estate planning can be a risky business, given the complex maze of property, tax, inheritance, and probate laws that govern estate planning. Even a seemingly small error or oversight can have very bad consequences for you and your loved ones. Therefore, more often than not, preparing your own estate plan is a penny-wise and pound-foolish decision.

TAKE THIS TEST

Still not convinced that working with an estate planning attorney is probably the best approach? Then complete the following true and false test. If you check *False* for even one statement, you need the help of a legal pro.

True _____ **False** _____ Your estate is very simple—you own very few assets, and they are not worth enough for estate taxes to be a concern. For example, you own a car, a modest home, and a small IRA; you have a couple thousand dollars in your checking account and a couple more in savings. Do not prepare your own plan if your estate includes business interests, income-generating property, and other complex assets.

True _____ **False** _____ Your estate is not worth enough that you need to be concerned about the amount of federal estate taxes that will be owed when you die. Deciding the best way to minimize those taxes and implementing an effective tax minimization strategy is always best left to a pro.

True _____ **False** _____ Your family situation is straightforward. You enjoy good relationships with all of your children, you and your spouse are not estranged, you are not married with children from a previous marriage, you do not intend to disinherit any of your children, none of your beneficiaries are mentally or physically disabled, and so on.

True _____ **False** _____ You are a single or married heterosexual. Estate planning for same-sex partners is complicated even if you live in a state that gives you and your partner some of the same inheritance rights that heterosexual spouses enjoy.

True _____ **False** _____ You are not interested in putting legally binding terms or conditions on any of the assets you are leaving to your beneficiaries. For example, you do not want to restrict your spouse's access to the assets that you are going to leave to him or her.

True _____ **False** _____ You don't want to include a testamentary trust in your will, and you are not interested in setting up a living trust. A trust is a complicated legal entity, especially a living trust, which must be set up exactly right for it to achieve your goals. There are many different types of trusts, and figuring out which one or combination of them is right for you can be tricky.

True _____ **False** _____ You are a self-disciplined person who will do all of the up-front research and organization essential to preparing an effective and legally enforceable estate plan. This includes boning up on the property laws in your state, creating a written inventory of all of your assets and debts, figuring out exactly how you own each asset, establishing your estate planning goals, and figuring out the best ways to achieve them through your plan.

True _____ **False** _____ You are not a procrastinator. If you are, you'll always find something "better" to do with your time than to prepare your estate plan, despite your best intentions. Don't forget, more than half of all Americans die without an estate plan.

True _____ **False** _____ You believe that there is no possibility that someone will contest your will after your death. A contest will cost your estate money—maybe a lot of money—because the court will appoint an attorney to represent your estate at the hearing(s) that will be held to resolve the contest. In addition, the hearings may be emotionally difficult for your loved ones, and none of the assets in your will can be transferred to your beneficiaries until the contest is resolved, which could create financial problems for your family. As a result of the contest, your will may be tossed out. If that happens, a judge will decide who ends up with your assets.

Resources for Writing Your Own Estate Plan

Resources are available for writing your own estate plan, but even if you do decide to prepare it yourself, it's a very good idea to purchase an hour or two of an estate planning attorney's time first. An attorney can help you make certain that you're absolutely clear about the estate planning and property laws of your state and that you haven't overlooked anything that could create problems for you and/or your loved ones down the road. It's possible that after meeting with an attorney, you may decide that preparing your estate plan is going to be far more complicated than you realized and that you really do need professional help.

It's also a good idea to meet with an estate planning attorney *after* you've completed your plan. Ask the attorney to review all of your documents to make sure that they are legally enforceable and that you've covered

If you are using will-writing software, make sure that it is either specific to your state or that it allows you to customize your documents to meet your state's requirements for a legally valid will.

all your bases. You should know, however, that some estate planning attorneys do not review do-it-yourself documents.

The following sections outline the three basic ways to prepare your own estate plan.

Estate Planning Software

You can purchase estate planning software online, at a bookstore, or at a computer or office supply store. If you are using will-writing software, make sure that it is either specific to your state or that it allows you to customize your documents to meet your state's requirements for a legally valid will. Also, be sure that the software is not so generic that it doesn't allow you to address your particular estate planning needs and concerns.

Use Fill-in-the-Blank Forms

You can download estate planning forms from the Internet, or you can purchase them at an office supply store. Also, some estate planning books include fill-in-the-blank forms. Make sure that the forms are specific to your state. Otherwise, your plan documents won't be legally valid when you die, and it will be as though you never prepared them. Also, be aware that you won't be able to customize the forms to address any special issues or concerns you may have related to your estate plan. Therefore, fill-in-the-blank forms are only appropriate when your estate and your wishes are very simple and straightforward.

Write Every Word of the Documents in Your Estate Plan Yourself

You can model your documents after sample documents you may find in a book or online. Although this particular approach provides you with the maximum amount of planning flexibility, it's a very risky option. You'll need to take every precaution possible to make sure that all of your words are clear and precise, and that you comply with every one of your state's requirements in order to end up with legally valid documents.

How an Estate Planning Attorney Can Help

If you decide to leave the preparation of your estate plan to a pro, your estate planning attorney can:

- **Educate you about how various property and estate planning laws relate to you and your estate.** Although books like this one, as well as estate planning websites and software, can provide you with a basic understanding of these laws, they can't address every legal nuance, nor can they completely explain how a specific law might apply to your particular situation. Your will must go through probate before any of your beneficiaries can receive the assets that you've left to them, and your attorney can work with you to minimize the number of assets that will go through that process.
- **Help you define and clarify your estate planning goals.** Your goal may be to make sure that your surviving spouse or partner has everything he or she needs to live a financially secure life after you're gone. Other goals may include ensuring that certain assets end up with the children from your prior marriage after your current spouse becomes deceased, avoiding probate, minimizing your estate taxes, and so on.
- **Determine the exact value of your estate.** If your estate is so large that it will owe federal estate taxes when you die, your attorney will help figure out ways to minimize the amount of those taxes.

Your will must go through probate before any of your beneficiaries can receive the assets that you've left to them, and your attorney can work with you to minimize the number of assets that will go through that process.

The right estate planning attorney for you is one who combines affordability with the right experience.

■ **Advise you about the pros and cons of making a will or a living trust the cornerstone of your estate plan.** Your attorney will explain what to consider in light of your goals, your finances, and your family situation.

■ **Help you coordinate your life insurance, retirement accounts, and other kinds of estate planning assets with the rest of your plan.** It's important that all the pieces of your plan work together to achieve your goals.

■ **Raise issues that you haven't thought through or that, if left unaddressed, could create problems for your loved ones after your death or incapacitation.** This could include legal and/or financial problems, some of which could have serious emotional ramifications for your loved ones. Estate planning attorneys can also advise you about what any potential debt would mean to your estate.

Finding a Good Estate Planning Attorney

The right estate planning attorney for you is one who combines affordability with the right experience. For example, if you are pretty certain that you want to build your estate plan on a will, then it doesn't make sense to hire an attorney who specializes in living trusts.

The best way to find the right attorney for you is to develop a list of estate planning attorneys in your area, narrow down the number of attorneys on that list to a manageable size, and then schedule meetings so you can ask each of them questions. Listen to their answers, observe their demeanor, and watch how they respond to you. Suggested questions to ask the attorneys you meet with are provided later in this chapter, together with information about what to watch and listen for during each meeting.

Developing an Attorney List

There are many ways to develop your attorney list. The following suggestions will help you generate a comprehensive list that meets your individual needs.

Talk with friends and family members who have already used an estate planning attorney and who were happy with their attorney. Try to get attorney referrals from people whose finances are similar to yours. For example, the estate planning attorney who helped your rich Uncle Bob deal with his millions will not be the right person for you if your estate is very modest.

Ask any non-estate planning attorneys you may know if they can recommend some estate planning attorneys in your area. Most attorneys will have some idea who the good ones are.

Talk with any financial professionals you may work with. They may include your banker, financial planner, CPA, insurance agent, or stockbroker.

Call your local or state bar association for some referrals to estate planning attorneys in your area. You can obtain the numbers to call using directory assistance or by checking your local yellow pages. You can also obtain contact information at the bar associations' websites.

If your state certifies attorneys in estate planning, when you contact your local or state bar association, ask for referrals to board-certified attorneys. Board

Try to get attorney referrals from people whose finances are similar to yours.

certification means that an attorney has a special interest in estate planning, has taken extra courses on the subject beyond what he or she learned in law school, has passed a rigorous state certification exam, and is committed to improving his or her estate planning skills and knowledge. A board-certified attorney must maintain his or her certification by taking periodic state-sponsored classes and seminars on the subject. At the time this book was written, Arizona, California, Florida, Louisiana, New Mexico, North Carolina, South Carolina, and Texas all offered certification.

However, being state-board certified and being referred by a bar association does not guarantee that a particular attorney will be right for you.

Find attorneys online. You can locate estate planning attorneys in your area by visiting the websites of estate planning attorney organizations like the American Academy of Estate Planning Attorneys (*www.aaepa.com*), the American College of Trust and Estate Counsel (*www.actec.org*), and the National Network of Estate Planning Attorneys (*www.nnepa.com*). Other helpful websites include Lawyers.com (*www.lawyers.com*), Martindale (*www.martindale.com*), and AttorneyFind (*www.attorneyfind.com*).

Talk to the trust department of your bank or to a local trust company if you are looking for an attorney who can help you set up a living trust. Trust officers regularly work with attorneys who specialize in living trust estate planning, so they should know who the best ones are.

Whittling Down the List

Once you have the names of some estate planning attorneys, you should take these next steps to condense your list so that it includes only the best candidates.

Visit the attorneys' websites. Do the sites appear professional and are they informative? Does anything about a particular site make you feel uncomfortable? Do the service descriptions at each site emphasize the particular services you are seeking? For example, if you're not in the market for a living trust or if estate taxes are not an issue for you, then you can scratch from your list any attorneys whose sites emphasize their living trust or tax minimization experience.

When you visit their websites, read each attorney's bio. Has the attorney been practicing estate planning law for at least five years—enough time to allow the attorney to start honing his or her skills? Is the attorney state-board certified in estate planning law, assuming your state offers such a certification?

Check your local yellow pages. Some of the attorneys on your list may have purchased display ads. If they have, are their ads in good taste?

Call the offices of each attorney, and ask to be sent information about the attorney's fees and services. If any of the offices tell you that they have nothing to send or refuse to send you what you've asked for, scratch that attorney from your list.

Once you've set up your appointments, prepare for them by thinking about your estate planning goals and any concerns you would like to discuss with the attorneys.

Contact your state bar association to confirm that each of the attorneys on your list is in good standing. Find out whether grievances have been filed against any of the attorneys recently and whether any of the attorneys ever had their license to practice law suspended.

Preparing for One-on-One Meetings with Attorneys

After you've whittled down your list to just a handful of attorneys, it's time to meet with each one. Call their offices, and explain that you are in the process of choosing an estate planning attorney and would like to schedule an appointment to meet with him or her in person. While you are on the phone, find out if you'll be charged for the meeting, and if you will, find out how much the meeting will cost. Most attorneys don't charge for an initial "getting to know you" meeting, but if any of the attorneys you contact do charge, and if the cost is more than you want to spend, then politely end your phone conversation.

When you set up your appointments, find out if there is any information that would be helpful for you to bring to your meetings. For example, you may be advised to bring the deeds to any real estate you own, the titles to your vehicles, copies of your life insurance policies, information about the value of your brokerage and retirement accounts, and so on. You also may be asked to bring your most recent tax returns and a list of all your assets and debts, among other things.

Once you've set up your appointments, prepare for them by thinking about your estate planning goals and any concerns you would like to discuss with the attorneys. In addition, prepare a written list of questions to ask each attorney. Having everything written out will help you make certain that you obtain all of the information you need to make an informed decision about which attorney to hire. Bring your list with you to each of your meetings, and don't be shy about also bringing a pad of paper or a notebook so you can jot down notes about what each attorney says, as well as your impressions of him or her.

Knowing What to Ask

When you prepare your list of questions, make sure that, at a minimum, you include the following.

- **How long have you been practicing estate planning law?** Although there is no magic number of years, it's best to hire an attorney who has been practicing estate planning law for at least five years. By that time, an attorney should have honed his or her skills and developed a good understanding of how to apply the information he or she learned in law school.

- **Based on what you know about my finances, my family, and my estate planning goals, what kind of plan do you think I need and why?**

- **What is your hourly rate and how do you charge for your services?** The attorneys should not only explain how much you can expect to pay for an estate plan, but they should also give you written information about their fees and expenses.

- **What factors might cause the cost of my estate plan to increase or decrease?**

- **Will you provide me with the names of some of your recent clients whose estate planning needs were similar to mine?** Try to get at least three references from each attorney, and then contact all references to find out if they were happy with the attorney they used and if they would hire that same attorney again. Don't work with an attorney who won't provide references.

Although there is no magic number of years, it's best to hire an attorney who has been practicing estate planning law for at least five years.

Never sign an agreement that you don't fully understand, and never work with an attorney who won't give you a copy of his or her agreement.

■ **Can I have a copy of the agreement that I will have to sign if I decide to hire you?** Take the agreement home so that you can read it at your leisure. If you have any questions about the agreement, get them answered by the attorney or one of the attorney's paralegals. Never sign an agreement that you don't fully understand, and never work with an attorney who won't give you a copy of his or her agreement.

If you are interested in a living trust, here are some additional questions you should ask.

■ **Do you prepare revocable living trusts?** If an attorney says yes, then ask the following questions next.

■ **About how many revocable living trusts do you prepare each year?** A good answer is at least 12—1 a month on average.

■ **Will you help me transfer to the trust all of the assets that I want in it?** The answer should be yes, because the process of legally transferring assets—called *funding* the trust—can be very time-consuming. If you try to do it yourself and don't finish the job, the assets that are not in the trust when you die will have to go through probate before they can be transferred to the trust.

■ **How will you create my living trust? Will you use software or will you create a customized trust agreement just for me?** If an attorney says that he or she will use living trust software, politely end the conversation. You want an attorney who will prepare most, if not all, of your living trust agreement from scratch, not someone who will simply plug your information into a software program and produce a generic living trust agreement. You can do that yourself with the right software!

Whether you are going to build your estate plan on a will or a living trust, be sure to find out how each attorney will help you keep your plan up-to-date. The best approach is for an attorney to schedule an annual meeting to review your estate plan and determine if it needs to be changed in any way.

Other Things to Consider When Choosing an Attorney

Besides considering how each attorney answers your questions and what an attorney's former clients have to say about him or her, you ought to take into account a few other things. Ask yourself the following questions after you meet with each attorney.

- Did the attorney act like your questions were silly or annoying?
- Did he or she act bored or uninterested in what you had to say?
- Did the attorney answer your questions in plain English, or did he or she use a lot of legal terms that left you wondering exactly what was meant?
- Did he or she ask you questions about your finances and your family to get a better idea about your estate planning needs?
- Did he or she seem more interested in selling you a living trust than in helping you figure out if you really need one?

Finally, don't ignore the chemistry between you and each of the attorneys you meet with. Remember, during the estate planning process, you will have to share private details about your life, some of which you may feel are embarrassing. Here are some examples: One of your children is in prison, you don't trust your spouse, your adult children from a prior marriage don't get along with your current spouse, or you haven't spoken to your middle child in five years. Also, many people don't like to talk about their finances, but you'll have to share every detail with your attorney. For all of these reasons, it's important to hire an attorney who makes you feel comfortable and who you can open up to.

Once You've Hired an Attorney

After you've chosen the estate planning attorney you want to work with, he or she will ask you to fill out a number of detailed forms that provide much of the information needed to begin your estate plan. You may have already pulled together some of the information requested when you were preparing to choose an attorney. Among other things, your attorney's forms will ask you about the following.

- Your age, employment, and health status
- Your marital status—married, divorced, separated, or widowed. If you are divorced, your attorney will want to see your divorce agreement.
- Whether you and your current spouse have a prenuptial or a postnuptial agreement. If you have, your attorney will want to see copies of each document.
- Whether you have an unmarried partner that you want to include in your plan and if you are in a same-sex relationship
- The composition of your family, including whether you have children from your current or any former marriages, whether you have stepchildren and/or grandchildren, their ages, and so on

- Information about the professional financial advisors you may be working with, including your banker, insurance agent, CPA, broker, and financial planner, among others
- All of your assets, including your real property, as well as your personal property such as bank, retirement, and investment accounts, life insurance policies, business interests, and so on. Your attorney will also want to see all of your deeds and titles and other ownership paperwork related to any assets that you own, including business assets, your life insurance policies, and so on.
- Your debts, including how much you owe and to whom you owe it
- Whether you've already prepared any estate planning documents. If you have, your attorney will want to see those documents, including any will, codicils (amendments to a will), living trust agreements, powers of attorney, and advance directives.

This chapter provided you with an overview of your do-it-yourself estate planning options, together with the pros and cons of each option. It should be apparent that, given the many complex and sometimes confusing laws that relate to estate planning, it's almost always best to work with an estate planning attorney. Among other things, an attorney can help you define and clarify your estate planning goals, think through the best way to achieve them, prepare and implement your plan, and make certain that it leaves nothing to chance. The step-by-step process for finding a good estate planning attorney provided in this chapter should get you on the right track.

Among other things, an attorney can help you define and clarify your estate planning goals, think through the best way to achieve them, prepare and implement your plan, and make certain that it leaves nothing to chance.

Estate Planning Tools

Will Power

**W**hen most people prepare their estate plan, they use a will to designate who they want to inherit their assets when they die. As explained in Chapter 1, a will is a legally binding statement (almost always a written statement) of who you want your assets to go to after you die. The following is an overview of the basic elements in a legally binding will.

Anatomy of a Will

Generally, all wills include the following information.

- Your name. Use the name that you use when you sign legal documents.
- Your address at the time that you write your will
- A statement that you are of sound mind and that the will is yours
- A clause revoking all previous wills or codicils (amendments to a will)
- The name of your current spouse and the names of all of your previous spouses, if any. If you have been married before, you should indicate for each spouse

Chapter 4

how the marriage ended—divorce, a legal annulment, or death.

■ The names of all of your children, if you have any, and each of their birth dates

■ The name of your will executor, information regarding whether your executor must post a bond, and the specific powers you are giving to him or her

■ The names of each of your beneficiaries and the specific assets you are leaving to each one

■ The name of your residuary beneficiary(ies) who will receive any assets in your estate that you haven't specifically left to someone else

■ The names of your trust beneficiary(ies), assuming you are including a trust in your will, as well as the name of the trustee and the provisions of the trust

■ The names of your children's personal and property guardians, if you have minor children

■ Your signature and the date on which you signed the will

■ The names and addresses of your witnesses

What a Will Can Do for You

As you will see in the following sections, you can do many things with a will beyond indicating who you want your assets to go to after you die.

Provide for the Establishment of a Testamentary Trust

A *testamentary trust* is a kind of trust created after your death. A will that includes a testamentary trust is referred to as a *complex will*. A will that doesn't is called a *simple will*. In your will, you'll indicate the assets that you want transferred to the trust and who you want to benefit from them. In addition, you can put terms and conditions on when and if your trust beneficiaries can have direct control over the trust assets and what they can do with them. The "Nailing Things Down with a Testamentary Trust" section of this chapter provides more details about testamentary trusts.

Designate the Adult You Want to Raise Your Minor Children

If you die while your children are still legal minors, which in most states means children who are younger than 18 years of age, you can use your will to designate which adult will raise them. This person is called your children's *personal guardian*. In fact, a will is the *only* legal means you have for designating this person. Therefore, if you don't prepare a will and you die with young children, a probate judge will decide who will raise them.

Designate a Property Guardian for Your Minor Children

If you leave assets directly to your young children in your will, you must indicate the adult whom you want to manage that property on your children's behalf. Legally, minor children can only own a very small amount of assets without an adult being in control of their property. If you fail to designate a *property guardian* for your children, a probate judge will name one for you.

Disinherit One of Your Children

When you disinherit a child, you leave him or her out of your will. You may decide to do that because you and your child are estranged from one another, you don't approve of the way your child is living his or her life, and so on. If you want to disinherit one of your children, it's best to work with an estate planning attorney to minimize the likelihood that, after your death, the child will

If you leave assets directly to your young children in your will, you must indicate the adult whom you want to manage that property on your children's behalf.

**Though you can
do a lot of things
with your will,
there are a lot of
things that you
can't do with it as
well.**

successfully contest the validity of your will and receive
some of your assets after all. Contesting the will slows
down the probate process and costs your estate money.
The "Will Contests: How They Work and How to Ward
Them Off" section of this chapter offers advice about
avoiding a will contest.

Forgive Any Debts That You May Be Owed

You can use your will to forgive any outstanding debts
that you may be owed. If you do not forgive them, your
executor will try to collect the debts after your death.

Limits to What a Will Can Do

Though you can do a lot of things with your will, there
are a lot of things that you *can't* do with it as well. The following are some of the things you can't use your will for.

Give Away Assets That You Don't Own

Those assets might include your spouse's half of your
community property, your spouse's separate property,
assets you've already given to someone else as an inter
vivos gift, and assets that you've transferred to a living
trust. You can only give away the assets that belong just
to you.

Give Away Assets That Automatically Transfer to Others "Outside" Your Will

Those assets include property that you own with someone else as joint tenants with the right of survivorship
or with your spouse as tenants in the entirety, your life
insurance policy death benefits, the funds in your 401(k)
or IRA, and other kinds of beneficiary accounts.

Limit Your Beneficiaries' Access to the Assets in Your Will and/or Put Terms and Conditions on Those Assets

You must either establish a testamentary trust inside your will or living trust outside your will in order to do those things.

Disinherit Your Spouse

Although you can disinherit your adult children, disinheriting your spouse is a different story. In most states you cannot do that because of something called the *elective share*, which entitles your surviving spouse to a minimum share of the value of the assets in your will—one-third of the value in most states, but one-half in others. In some states, surviving spouses are entitled not only to a minimum share of the assets in the will of their deceased spouse, but also to a minimum share of their spouse's joint tenancy assets and any assets the deceased spouse may have transferred to a living trust.

If you live in a community property state, your spouse can't be disinherited because he or she legally owns one-half of the value of all the assets from your marriage. However, nothing prevents you from leaving your half to someone other than your spouse.

Transfer Property to Your Pet

Your pet cannot own property. So if you want to be sure that Fido or Fluffy will be well cared for after your death, a better alternative is to leave the assets you've earmarked for your pet to an animal-loving friend or relative, together with specific instructions for how you want the money spent. Of course, you may want to set up a trust for your pets so that they can live in the lap of luxury after your death.

You can't use your assets to encourage your beneficiaries to engage in any sort of illegal activity.

Encourage One of Your Beneficiaries to Do Something Illegal

You can't use your assets to encourage your beneficiaries to engage in any sort of illegal activity. For example, you can't leave money to a beneficiary and direct that it be spent on illegal gambling, a marijuana-growing business, and so on.

Make a Beneficiary's Receipt of His or Her Inheritance Contingent on That Person's Actions

For example, you can't generally prohibit one of your beneficiaries from receiving the assets you left to him or her in your will unless that person gets a divorce, changes political parties, begins practicing a particular religion, and so on.

Give Instructions for Your Burial or Cremation

Also, although no law prohibits you from leaving instructions for your burial or cremation and memorial service in your will, it's not a good idea because it's possible that no one will read your will until after those events have taken place. A better option is to write a letter expressing your wishes and to give your executor a copy of the letter. You will probably want to give a copy to your spouse or partner and maybe to your adult children, as well. Let everyone know where your letter is stored and, if it's in your home safe or a safe-deposit box, instructions on how they can access it. Another option is to include your instructions in your durable medical power of attorney document. Chapter 10 discusses this kind of legal document in detail.

Writing a Legally Enforceable Will

Every will must meet certain state requirements in order to be legally valid. If you write your own and it doesn't meet your state's requirements, then the wishes you've expressed in it won't be enforceable. It will be as though you never wrote a will.

In most states, for your will to be legally valid:

- **It must be typed** on a computer or typewriter, although some states accept other kinds of wills.
- **You must have been at least 18 years of age** when you wrote it. However, a few states—Georgia and Louisiana—permit someone younger than 18 to write a will. Most states, however, allow someone who is younger than 18 to write a legally valid will only if he or she is married, economically independent, or in the armed services.
- **You must have been of sound mind** when you wrote it. In other words, you were capable of understanding the significance of what you were doing, you were aware of the nature of your assets (real estate, a boat, a car, for example), and you were clear about to whom you were leaving your property.
- **It must reflect *your* wishes**, not someone else's. For example, your will won't be legally valid if someone can prove to the court that you were coerced into including certain provisions in it—for example, your younger brother pressured you into leaving all of your assets to him.
- **It must be dated and you must have signed it** in front of two legally competent adult witnesses (three in some states). They cannot be beneficiaries of your will.
- **It *must* be notarized.**

WILLS COME IN DIFFERENT FORMS

Although a typed will is the gold standard in all states, some states recognize other kinds of wills under certain circumstances. Those other kinds of wills are:

- **Oral or *nuncupative* wills.** You create this kind of will simply by stating your wishes in the presence of someone else. Few states recognize oral wills, however, and those that do only recognize them in very narrowly defined circumstances. For example, when you're on your deathbed. Also, states that recognize oral wills typically limit the total value of property that they can transfer.

- **Handwritten or *holographic* wills.** About half the states recognize this kind of will, assuming that it's been signed and dated. Most states don't require that this kind of will be witnessed. However, it's never a good idea to prepare a handwritten will. One reason why it's a bad idea is that if your penmanship is bad, your wishes may be misinterpreted or a probate judge may throw out your will because no one can read what you wrote. Another reason is that it's relatively easy to alter a handwritten will.

- **Electronic wills.** Presently, only Nevada recognizes the validity of electronic wills. They may become more widely accepted in the future.

- **Video wills.** You create this kind of will by stating your wishes out loud in front of a video camera. Presently, however, no states recognize video wills. More often than not they are used as a backup to a typed will when there is a concern that someone may try to contest the will by claiming that the will maker was incompetent when he or she wrote it. The thinking is that the video would help prove otherwise.

Joint Wills and Spouses Don't Always Mix

If you are married or have a same-sex partner, it's unwise to share a will with your spouse or partner. You should each prepare your own separate will. The reason is that your state is likely to treat your joint will as a binding contract between the two of you. As a result, when one of you dies the surviving spouse can't revise or revoke the joint will, no matter how out-of-date it might become.

When you prepare separate wills, however, you will probably want to coordinate them to some degree. For example, if you live in a community property state, be sure that you both leave your individual shares of your marital assets to the same beneficiary(ies). If you have minor children, you will probably want to designate the same individual(s) to be their personal guardian and their property guardian, if you plan to pass on your assets to your children through your wills.

Now Comes the Good Part: Giving Your Stuff Away!

Writing your will gives you the chance to play Santa Claus. You get to leave your assets to whomever you want! So get out your asset inventory, identify the assets you own that you can transfer through your will, and start thinking about to whom you want to leave them.

Your decision may be a no-brainer, especially if you don't have much to give away in the first place. When that's the case, you'll probably leave most, if not all, of your significant assets to your surviving spouse (or partner) and make your children, if you have any, the secondary or alternate beneficiaries of your will. This means that they will inherit all of the assets you've left to your spouse if he or she is already deceased when you die, or if your spouse is still alive at that point but does not survive you by a certain number of days (you must specify the number in your will). Forty-five or 90 days is typical.

If you don't have a spouse or partner and/or if you have no children, then choosing your beneficiaries may be a bigger challenge, especially if your estate is substantial. You may decide to leave all of your assets to your surviving siblings and make their children your alternate beneficiaries, you may leave everything to your nieces and nephews and nothing to your siblings, or you may decide to divide your estate up among relatives, friends, and your favorite charities. It's up to you.

To help you think about what to do, ask yourself the following questions.

Do I want to leave everything I own to my spouse or partner? You may not if your spouse or partner has plenty of his or her own assets and doesn't need any of yours to live a comfortable life after you die. Perhaps you've already made your spouse or partner the beneficiary of your retirement accounts, life insurance policy, and/or other beneficiary accounts, or you've set up a living trust to benefit him or her.

If I leave my estate to my spouse or partner, will I create a future estate tax problem for him or her? If this is a concern, an estate planning attorney can help you decide how to avoid this problem.

Do I want to leave my share of my community property to my surviving spouse? If you don't, be cautious about whom you leave it to because that person will end up owning that property with your spouse, and you may unwittingly create problems for them as a result. For example, your spouse and his or her co-owner(s) may not see eye to eye on how to manage their joint property, may not agree on whether it should be sold, whether to borrow against it, and so on. These disagreements could create financial as well as legal problems for your surviving spouse after your death, and could add a lot of stress and worry to his or her life.

Is my spouse or partner a good money manager? Does he or she have a spending problem? It's never wise to leave a substantial amount of assets directly to anyone who can't manage them responsibly and/or who is an impulsive spender, because that person may squander every penny and not have enough to live on as a result. Here's a better approach: Set up a testamentary trust in your will for the benefit of your spouse or partner, and put someone you trust in charge of the assets that will be transferred to the trust. Direct that person—the trustee of the trust—to pay all of your spouse or partner's living expenses and debts, and to provide him or her with a monthly or weekly stipend. Protecting your spouse or partner in this way is a loving thing to do. Another way to do the same thing is to set up a living trust outside your will for the benefit of your surviving spouse or partner.

Do I want to treat all of my adult children exactly the same way in my will? Though most people do, it may make sense to treat them differently. For example, one of your children may have had an especially difficult life and so you may want to give him or her a financial helping hand through your will; you may have already given one of your children a significant amount of money, so you may see no need to give that child much more of what you own; or one of your children may be very successful and have more money than what he or she knows what to do with.

If you decide to treat your children differently in your will, it's a good idea to provide a clear explanation in your will of why you have made that decision. Also, explaining your decision to your children while you are alive may help minimize the possibility that any of them

> If you decide to treat your children differently in your will, it's a good idea to provide a clear explanation in your will of why you have made that decision.

will be hurt by your decision, strike out in anger at the other siblings, or try to contest your will.

Do I want my children to have full control over the assets that I am leaving to them in my will? The answer may be no, especially if there is a good chance that your children will be young adults when you die and will inherit a substantial amount of property from you at that point. You may be concerned that, if they have control over that property before they are mature enough to manage it responsibly, they will waste their inheritance, lose their motivation to succeed in life, and so on. Transferring their assets to a testamentary trust or a living trust are the best ways to address these concerns. Estate planning for your children is discussed more fully in Chapter 9.

Have I promised anyone that I will leave him or her anything in particular in my will? If you have, you should either do what you said you would or give that person something else that you know he or she will also value. In addition, you should let that person know what you've done so there will be no unpleasant surprises and hurt feelings when your will is read.

Is any aspect of my will likely to create conflict among my loved ones when I die and/or cause my will to be contested? It's smart to discuss your concerns with an estate planning attorney. He or she will provide you with advice about what you can do now to head off problems later. For example, if you've decided to disinherit one of your children, your attorney will advise you about the steps you should take now to minimize the likelihood that the child will contest your decision after your death. "Will Contests: How They Work and How to Ward Them Off" at the end of this chapter offers some advice.

Who will I designate as my residual beneficiary?
When you write your will, be sure to designate a residual beneficiary and an alternate in your will. This is the person (or organization) who will receive whatever may be left in your probate estate after your estate has paid all probate-related fees and expenses and any debts and taxes you may owe, and after all of the assets you have left to specific beneficiaries have been distributed. The assets that are left over may include property you forgot to include in your will, as well as assets that you may have acquired after you wrote your will. If you don't designate a residual beneficiary and an alternate, the probate judge will decide who gets such assets.

Also, don't forget about the "small stuff" when you are writing your will. As Chapter 2 explained, some members of your family may have sentimental attachments to some of the things that you own that are relatively insignificant from a financial perspective, like your mother's cookie jar or your favorite rocking chair. You may want to give these items away while you are alive or through your will, or you may decide to use some other means to distribute the "small stuff."

Nailing Things Down with a Testamentary Trust

As already explained, a testamentary trust is a kind of trust that you create through your will for the benefit of one or more beneficiaries. You will designate these beneficiaries in your will. Because the trust is a part of your will, it won't come into existence until after your death, and the assets that you want to be in the trust won't be transferred to it until after the probate process has begun. In your will you may identify specific assets that you want placed in the trust, or you may direct that all or some of your residuary assets be transferred to the

Also, don't forget about the "small stuff" when you are writing your will.

While you are alive, you can change the assets that will be transferred to the trust, the trust beneficiaries, the trustee, and so on.

trust. Another way to fund the trust is to purchase a life insurance policy and to make the trust the policy beneficiary. Then, when you die, the policy death benefits are paid to the trust.

In your will you must also indicate who the trustee of the trust will be. This person will manage the trust assets according to the terms and conditions that you set out. You may give the trustee total decision-making discretion, little discretion, or something in between.

While you are alive, you can change the assets that will be transferred to the trust, the trust beneficiaries, the trustee, and so on. After you die, however, everything about the trust is set in stone.

Reasons to include a testamentary trust in your will include:

- To reduce the amount of estate taxes your surviving spouse will owe upon his or her death.
- To protect your spouse or partner from him or herself. This might be appropriate if your spouse knows little or nothing about money management, has an addiction, is overly trusting and gullible, cannot say no to your children no matter what they ask for, and so on.
- To control when and if your children will have access to the assets that you are leaving to them and what they can do with those assets. You may worry that receiving a substantial inheritance as young adults will cause your children to lose their motivation to get a college education, to work hard, and to be productive citizens. Also, if your children are already adults when you prepare your plan, you may not think it's a good idea for some of them to have full control over their inheritance if they have addiction problems, have shown themselves to be irresponsible

with money, and so on. When you leave assets directly to your children through your will, they will gain full control over these assets as soon as they become legal adults—18 years old in most states.

■ To provide lifetime care for your seriously disabled child without jeopardizing his or her eligibility for government benefits, including Supplemental Security Income, Medicaid, and low-income housing.

If you're thinking about including a testamentary trust in your will, always work with an estate planning attorney. Trusts are complicated! Also, find out whether your attorney thinks that a living trust might be a better way to achieve your estate planning objectives—they can achieve goals that testamentary trusts can't.

Although testamentary trusts are less expensive than living trusts to set up, they have some disadvantages. For example, the assets you want transferred to a testamentary trust must go through probate, which means that they won't be immediately available to your trust beneficiaries. In fact, depending on how quickly your estate is probated, it could be months, if not years, before your beneficiaries actually benefit from the assets. In addition, the assets will increase the cost of probate for your estate, and all of the trust details will be a part of the public record.

Your Young Children and Your Will

If you have minor children, you'll have two very important decisions to make when you write your will. The first is who you'll name as their property guardian. This is assuming that you intend to leave assets to them directly, as opposed to transferring the assets to a testamentary

KIPLINGER'S ESTATE PLANNING

trust after your death or to a custodial account for each child (custodial accounts are discussed in Chapter 7). Their property guardian will manage these assets on your children's behalf until they become legal adults.

The second decision is who you'll name as your children's personal guardian. This is the person they will live with and who will fill your shoes as a parent. The responsibilities of this person will end once your children reach the age of adulthood. At that point, your kids will be on their own.

Figuring Out Who'll Manage Your Kids' Assets

Young children are only allowed to own a very minimal amount of property. The amount varies from state to state, but in most states the value is between $2,500 and $5,000. Also, children cannot sell their assets, borrow against them, open a bank or brokerage account, or enter into binding contracts related to their assets. They need an adult to do those things for them. Therefore, if you leave your children more than the minimum amount of assets in your will, be sure to carefully choose the adult who will manage those assets for them. This person is called a property guardian. Designate an alternate property guardian, too.

In addition to managing the assets you've left to your kids in your will, the property guardian will also manage any assets they may inherit if you've made them the beneficiaries of your life insurance policy, retirement accounts, brokerage accounts, and so on. Also, the property guardian will need to work closely with your children's personal guardian to ensure that, as much as possible, the personal guardian has the financial resources necessary to raise your children—to buy their food, purchase their clothes, provide for their medical care, and pay for their school supplies and extracurricular activities—all of the things that you and your spouse or partner pay for now.

Most people name their surviving spouse or partner, another family member, or a close friend to be their children's property guardian. Many people make their children's personal guardian their property guardian too, because that arrangement is very convenient. However, you may not know anyone who has the temperament and skills to raise children and who has the knowledge and ability to manage their financial assets as well.

If you don't choose the same person to play both roles in the lives of your children, it's a good idea to be clear in your will about your expectations for each, including how these two people should communicate and cooperate with one another. It's also wise to have a face-to-face meeting with both guardians to discuss your expectations and any concerns they may have.

If you don't think that anyone you know will make a good property guardian for your children, you can choose a professional for the job. However, his or her fees and expenses, which could be considerable, will come out of the assets that you've left to your kids.

The Probate Court and Property Guardians

Your children's property guardian will be supervised by a probate court in your state and will have to adhere to the following rules.

Get the court's approval before making certain kinds of expenditures. However, you can minimize the potential for problems in this regard by spelling out in your will the kinds of "extras" you want your kids to

Your children's personal guardian will have all of the same legal rights and responsibilities that you have as a parent.

have, assuming there is enough money—private school, summer camp, tutoring, and mental health counseling, for example. If you don't, it's possible that the judge may refuse to let the property guardian pay for many of the things that were a normal part of your children's lives while you were alive.

Account for what he or she does with your children's assets. The property guardian must do this by filling out detailed periodic reports with the court. Theoretically, the reports are supposed to protect your children by alerting the court to problems (mismanagement or malfeasance on the part of their property guardian) so that it can step in. In reality, however, the reports probably won't be closely read or read on a timely basis.

Also, the guardian must purchase a bond from a bonding company and post it with the court. The bond will protect your children in the event that their property guardian misuses, wastes, or steals the assets you left to them by repaying them for their loss. The amount of the bond will depend on the size of your children's inheritance. In some states, the property guardian may be able to post a letter of credit from a bank or put up some of their own property rather than post a bond.

You can waive the bonding requirement in your will if you want. You might decide to waive it because you don't want the relative or friend who has agreed to be your children's property guardian to have to incur the expense of getting bonded, and because you totally trust that person to do a good job of managing your children's assets.

Deciding Who Will Fill Your Shoes as a Parent

Your children's personal guardian will have all of the same legal rights and responsibilities that you have as a parent. For example, he or she will make decisions about their food and clothing, medical care, schooling, religion, and after-school and summer activities. The personal guardian will also be responsible for how your children will be disciplined, the values they will be raised with, how often they will visit their grandparents and other relatives, and so on. Important stuff! Most people choose a relative or close friend as their children's personal guardian.

If you are like many parents, choosing a personal guardian for your kids will be extremely difficult because there probably isn't a perfect choice. It will likely be a balancing act and a judgment call on your part—what qualities do you think are most important for a personal guardian to have and who do you think will do the best job raising your kids?

To start making this decision, come up with a list of people who are possible candidates, and then evaluate each of them against the criteria that are most important to you. For example, as you are evaluating each person on your list, ask yourself if he or she is:

■ **Mature and levelheaded.**
■ **In a happy, stable relationship.**
■ **Financially stable and financially able to absorb your children into his or her household.** Ideally, you can provide their personal guardian with all of the money he or she needs to raise your kids, but if this isn't the case for you, then take into account whether raising your children will impose too big of a financial burden on the person you are considering. For example, can that person afford to buy a new home or a new car to accommodate your children?
■ **Young enough.** It's best if the person you choose as your children's personal guardian is young enough

that he or she will most likely be in their lives for years to come, or at least until they become legal adults. Therefore, it's usually not a good idea to designate one of their grandparents—although many of today's grandparents are active, vital people, and many of them are raising their grandchildren.

- **Similar to you in regard to mental outlook.** The mental outlook of your children's personal guardian will have a big effect on their lives and on their own outlook toward life.
- **Similar to you in regard to your values, priorities, and attitudes toward child rearing.**
- **Residing in your community.** This matters most if you don't want your children to be uprooted and have to leave the rest of their family, their friends, their school, and so on.
- **In good health.** A person with a lot of physical and/or emotional problems may not be a good choice, especially if your children are quite young, very active, or require a lot of chauffeuring from here to there.
- **Well-suited to raise your children.** Not every adult is cut out to be a parent. Raising children takes patience, self-sacrifice, nurturing, and lots of love.

You should also take into account whether the person:

- **Enjoys being around your kids and vice versa.** If they don't know one another right now, do you think they could learn to enjoy one another?
- **Has good relationships with his or her own children.** This can be a pretty accurate barometer of what that person's relationship with your kids will be like.
- **Has the time to raise your children.** Someone with young children of their own, who works long hours,

or who travels a lot, may be unable to give your kids the time and attention they need and deserve.

If you have preteens or teens, go ahead and ask them who they would like as their personal guardian. No doubt they will have opinions!

If the person you are considering is married, it's best just to name only him or her in your will, given the high percentage of marriages that end in divorce. If you name both spouses and then they get divorced, the issue of who will raise your children could end up in court. Even if the couple can make that decision for themselves, the court will still have to approve what they decide, and there is always the chance that it might not do so. If that were to happen, the court would designate a personal guardian for your kids.

Before you formally designate someone as personal guardian, get together with the person you want for that role, and make sure that he or she is willing to take on all of that responsibility. Talk frankly about the personalities and needs of each of your children, how you want them raised, the issues that you are most worried about, the kinds of financial resources you can provide to help him or her raise your children, and so on. Encourage the person you are meeting with to ask you questions, to express concerns, and to be totally honest with you about whether they want to be your children's personal guardian. Be clear that if he or she tells you no, there will be no hard feelings or recriminations on your part. You should have a similar conversation with whomever you want to name as an alternate personal guardian for your children. You may want to name a couple of alternates just to be safe.

The court must approve whomever you choose, so it's always a good idea to include a clear rationale for your choice in your will. For example, you may want to address the key factors that influenced your decision, how long you have know the person you want as your children's personal guardian, your relationship with one another, how well he or she knows your children, and so on. This information may be especially helpful if someone challenges your decision after your death.

If you are in a same-sex relationship and you and your partner are raising children together, be sure to take whatever steps are necessary to ensure that should you die, your partner will be legally entitled to raise them. For example, some states allow same-sex adoptions. A same-sex adoption would also mean that your children would be legally entitled to inherit from you as well as from your partner. At the time this book was written, Florida and New Hampshire have laws prohibiting such adoptions, and even in states without a legal prohibition, the process can be difficult. Talk with a family law attorney in your state about same-sex adoption. If your partner does not adopt your children, make sure that you designate him or her as their personal guardian, and provide plenty of information to support your decision. It's best to discuss with an estate planning attorney exactly what to say, especially if you know that some of your family members object to your same-sex relationship.

A Final Word of Advice When It Comes to Your Kids

When you are deciding who to designate as your children's property and personal guardians, it's best if you and their other parent can make these decisions together, and that you each designate the same individuals in your separate wills. If the two of you can't agree on who the guardians should be, consider using outside help to reach a decision. For example, you may want to consult your religious advisor or a mental health professional, or even try mediation. If you do nothing and the worst happens, it could be disastrous for your children because a probate judge—a total stranger—will decide who will raise them and who will manage their assets.

Once You've Got It All Down on Paper

Once your will is finished, but *before* you've signed it, make a copy for your executor (and alternate) and for anyone else you want to share it with, like your spouse or partner. Be sure to spend time reviewing everything in your will with your executor, so that he or she understands your wishes and so that you can answer any questions your executor may have about your will.

Store your signed and witnessed will (get it notarized too if that's a legal requirement in your state) in a secure, fireproof and waterproof place, like a safe-deposit box at your bank or home, your home safe, or at the office of your estate planning attorney. If you store it in your bank safe-deposit box, ask the bank or your estate planning attorney if access to the box will be restricted immediately after your death. Some states will seal the box or limit access to it until the probate process begins. Even so, lack of access or restricted access shouldn't be a problem because your bank will make your will available to your executor when he or she needs it, and because you should have already provided your executor with a copy of your will, so he or she can begin planning for the probate process.

Tell your executor, your spouse or partner, and at least one other person you trust where your will is stored. Also, be sure that if it's stored in a safe-deposit box at your home they have a key to the box and that if it's stored in your home safe, they know the combination. If you're storing it at the office of your attorney

Be sure to spend time reviewing everything in your will with your executor, so that he or she understands your wishes and so that you can answer any questions your executor may have about your will.

Review your will at least once a year, along with the rest of your estate planning documents, to make certain that it's up-to-date and continues to reflect your wishes.

or CPA, provide them with that person's address and contact information, including phone numbers and email addresses.

Changing Your Will

Review your will at least once a year, along with the rest of your estate planning documents, to make certain that it's up-to-date and continues to reflect your wishes. If you want to change anything in your will, you can formally amend it by preparing a will codicil or by writing a new will and canceling your old one.

Here are some examples of when you should either amend your will or write a new one.

- **You get divorced.** In some states, all provisions in your will that apply to your ex are automatically cancelled when your divorce is final, which means that you'll need to redistribute the assets that you left to your former spouse. A few states, however, will revoke your entire will, which means that once you're divorced, you will have no will.
- **You marry for the first time.** You'll almost certainly want to include your new spouse in your will.
- **You become widowed.** Like when you get divorced, you'll need to decide who will inherit the assets that would have gone to your spouse.
- **You have entered into a committed relationship with your same-sex partner.**
- **You and your spouse or partner have another child together or you adopt a child.**
- **You acquire new assets or you sell, give away, or lose assets that are in your current will.**
- **Some of the assets in your will have significantly appreciated in value or have lost value.** If either of

these things happen, you may want to redistribute your assets among your beneficiaries, taking into account the amount of the appreciation or loss. For example, if you want to treat all of your children exactly the same way in your will and some of the assets you've left to one child have gone up or down in value, then you'll need to revise your will to make up for the change. This won't be necessary if, rather than making specific bequests to your children, your will makes a general bequest that designates specific categories of assets to go in equal shares to all of your children.

Generally, if you are making a relatively small change to your will, it's fine to make it by preparing a *codicil*, which is legalese for a written statement of the change you are making. Your codicil should reference the specific provision in your will that the change applies to. Also, make sure that the codicil will be legally enforceable by signing it and by observing all of the other legal formalities that make a will legally valid in your state. Once you've completed your codicil, make copies of the document and give a copy to whoever has a copy of your will. Store the original with your will.

You can prepare your own codicil but, as with a will, if the document is not worded exactly right and doesn't comply with all of your state's requirements for a legally valid codicil, it won't be enforceable when you die. Therefore, it's always best to either hire an attorney to prepare your codicil or to review it if you draft your own.

If you're making significant changes to your will, however, it's best to write an entirely new will that contains a clause that specifically revokes all previous wills and codicils. A significant change might include a dramatic redistribution of your assets among your beneficiaries, disinheriting one of your adult children, or adding a testamentary trust to your will. If you write a new will, be sure to destroy all existing copies of your previous wills.

If you wrote your own will and you're not sure if you should revise it by preparing a codicil or by writing a new will, play it safe and prepare a new will. Otherwise, if you prepare a codicil when you should have written a new will instead, it's possible that when you die the probate court won't recognize the change that you made as legally valid, or you may leave your will open to a contest. If you want to be 100 percent sure about what to do, contact an estate planning attorney.

A word of warning: *Never* revise your will by scratching out the provisions that you want to change and writing in new provisions. In some states, if you do this you will invalidate your entire will.

Will Contests: How They Work and How to Ward Them Off

Although contests to a will can inspire exciting human dramas on TV, in the movies, or in a legal thriller, most wills are never contested. When there is a contest, it's usually unsuccessful. That's the good news. The bad news, however, is that if your will is contested, the contest will be resolved in a public courtroom, where all of your family's "dirty laundry" may be hung out to dry. Also, defending your will against the contest will cost your estate money—maybe a lot of it. Therefore, it's always best to write your will defensively, with one eye on the possibility that it may be contested. Here are some things you can do to help discourage a contest.

■ **While you are alive, let your immediate family members and anyone else who may be expecting to inherit**

from you know what is in your will. Also, explain why you've made the decisions you've made. Another option is to write letters to your beneficiaries and to your legal heirs, explaining the decisions you made when you wrote your will.

■ **Include an anticontest clause in your will.** The clause should state that anyone who contests your will automatically loses whatever you may have left to him or her in it. Don't forget to stipulate in your will what should happen to the forfeited gift.

■ **If you are leaving someone out of your will and are concerned that that person may contest your will as a result, leave him or her something.** This can be something small but significant enough to help discourage a contest. Another way to deal with this situation when it comes to any legal heirs that you intend to leave out of your will is to specifically mention each of them in your will and to specifically state that you are not leaving them anything. Doing so should help undercut anyone who tries to argue that you meant to leave something to him or her, but you forgot.

■ **Amend your will the right way, don't scratch things out and write things in.** Prepare a legally enforceable codicil, or write a new will and revoke your old one. As previously mentioned, in some states, if you scratch things out and/or write things in, it will invalidate your entire will.

■ **Use a legally binding prenuptial agreement.** In the agreement, you and your spouse-to-be can work out ahead of time exactly what you will and won't leave to each other in your wills. You can ask your future spouse to formally agree in the document not to contest your will. If you are married and you don't have a prenuptial agreement, you and your spouse can do the same things using a postnuptial agreement.

Generally, only someone who stands to gain something from your estate can contest your will.

Always prepare these agreements with the help of attorneys—one for you and one for your future or current spouse. If you have a same-sex partner, you can prepare similar agreements.

■ **Have a professional videographer videotape you signing your will and having it witnessed.** The video might also include footage of you answering questions about why you left someone out of your will, why you left a certain asset to a particular person, what you want your will to accomplish, and so on. The video can help prove that when you wrote your will, you were of sound mind, knew exactly what you were doing and why, and were not unduly influenced by anyone.

■ **Ask your doctor to write a letter.** The letter should state that the doctor examined you just prior to the date that you wrote your will and that you were in good health and of sound mind at that time. Keep the original letter with your will, and give a copy to your executor.

■ **Transfer your assets to a living trust.** Compared to a will, it's a lot harder to undo the provisions of a living trust.

Generally, only someone who stands to gain something from your estate can contest your will. Therefore, one of your legal heirs can contest your will, as well as anyone who would be affected somehow if the terms of your will were carried out. However, no one can contest your will on a whim—they have to have a legal basis for doing so. Furthermore, to win their contest they must prove to a judge that what they've alleged is true. Legal grounds for a will contest can include the following.

■ You were mentally incompetent when you wrote your will, so you didn't understand what you were doing.
■ You failed to execute your will according to the laws of your state.

- You were under undue influence when you wrote your will, so it doesn't reflect your true wishes. In other words, someone convinced you to put certain things in your will in order to gain something.
- You were tricked into signing your will. For example, someone deceived you into signing your will by misleading you about something in it or by making you think that what you were signing was a different document, not your will.

If someone formally contests your will, the probate process will be suspended, and a hearing on the contest will be scheduled. The hearing will involve your executor, the person who has filed the contest and his or her attorney, the attorney who is representing your estate, and the probate judge. If the contest is successful, either the specific provision in your will that was contested is tossed out or your entire will is invalidated. If the latter happens, all of the assets in your probate estate will be distributed to your legal heirs according to the intestacy law of your state. In other words, it will be as though you never wrote a will.

In this chapter, you found out what you can and can't accomplish with a will, about the basic kinds of information in most wills, how testamentary trusts work, and when you should revise your will or write a new one. You are now also aware what you can do to minimize the likelihood that someone will contest the details of your will after your death. If you are a parent of minor children, the importance of designating their personal guardian in your will should now be clear, as should some of the key issues you ought to consider when you are choosing this person. You should also now appreciate why you must name a property guardian for your young children if you are leaving them an inheritance in your will.

Your Will, Your Executor, and the Probate Process

If you use a will to transfer your assets when you die, the assets must go through a court-supervised legal process called probate before they can be distributed to the beneficiaries indicated in your will. A probate court judge oversees this process, and the person you've designated in your will as your executor will represent your *probate estate* during the process. Your probate estate is simply all of the assets that are being transferred through your will.

Duties of Your Executor

Your executor will act as the legal representative of your probate estate during the probate process. He or she will have a lot of duties and obligations during that process, and carrying out those responsibilities may be very time-consuming. Your executor is legally entitled to receive a fee for his or her services. The following is an overview of what your executor will be expected to do.

- **Locate your will.** The probate process cannot officially begin until your will has been located, so ideally your executor will know where it is stored and have immediate access to it.

■ **Complete a special petition form.** This form will be filed in the probate court in the county where you reside when you die. The petition asks the court to formally accept your will. If there are no objections, the probate court will formally appoint your executor and accept your will. In some states, however, before your will can be accepted and before your executor can be formally appointed, your executor must publish a legal notice in your local newspaper announcing that you have died. The notice must say that the petition has been filed, and specify a date by which anyone who wants to contest your will or the court's appointment of your executor can do so.

■ **Create a written inventory of all the assets in your probate estate, and determine a market value (current value) for each asset.** Your executor will take legal title to these assets. Your executor may have to hire appraisers and real estate professionals to accurately value some of your assets. Your estate will pay their fees.

■ **Notify your creditors about your death and of their right to file claims against your probate estate so that the debts that you owe to them can be paid.** Your creditors will have a limited amount of time to file their claims.

■ **Fill out and file a federal and a state tax return, and pay any estate taxes your estate may owe.** Those taxes must be paid before your executor can distribute any of your assets to your will beneficiaries. Some states have no estate tax.

■ **Try to collect any money your estate may be owed.** Doing so may require that your executor file lawsuits on behalf of your estate.

■ **Manage the property in your probate estate.** For example, you may own rental property or a closely held business. To manage your assets, your executor may need the assistance of various business professionals. Your estate will pay the cost of their assistance.

- **Pay your estate's other financial obligations.** These obligations include the following: your funeral expenses, unless you made other payment arrangements; your estate's administrative expenses, including your executor's fee (assuming your executor didn't waive the right to be paid for his or her services), the fees charged by the probate attorney your executor may have hired, and any costs associated with locating, valuing, and managing your assets; any federal or state estate taxes your estate may owe; and all legitimate debts you may owe at the time of your death. If your bank and money market accounts lack sufficient funds to pay all of your estate's financial obligations, your executor may have to sell some of your assets.

- **Help defend your will against any contests.** Fortunately, few wills are contested. However, if there are any contests, your executor will need to hire an attorney to defend your will against them. Also, the contests will delay the transfer of your assets to your beneficiaries.

- **Transfer the appropriate assets to your testamentary trust, if you included one in your will.**

- **Prepare a final written report for the probate court.** The report will detail all of the assets in your probate estate, as well as all of the income those assets may have earned since your death—from rental property, other investments, royalties, and so on. The report will also include everything that the executor paid out of your estate and how he or she plans to distribute what remains of your estate to your beneficiaries.

- **Distribute your assets according to the terms of your will.** This cannot happen, however, until all of your estate's taxes, fees, expenses, and debts have been

> If your bank and money market accounts lack sufficient funds to pay all of your estate's financial obligations, your executor may have to sell some of your assets.

Once your assets have been distributed, your estate will be closed, the probate process will be over, and your executor's job will be done.

paid, and all contests to your will and any objections to your executor's report have been resolved. Once your assets have been distributed, your estate will be closed, the probate process will be over, and your executor's job will be done.

- **Participate in an abatement process, if needed.** If your estate doesn't have enough money to pay all of your cash gifts, and your will includes no specific instructions about what to do in such a situation, your executor will have to participate in an *abatement process*. This process will be governed by the rules of your state, and it provides a means of addressing the shortfall, usually in one of two ways. Here's how the first way works: Your executor will sell any property that you haven't left to a specific beneficiary. If the sale proceeds are not enough to cover the cash short-fall, then your executor will sell some of the personal assets you left to specific beneficiaries in your will. If even more cash is needed, then your executor will sell some of the real property you gave away in your will. If your executor uses the other abatement method to raise enough funds to pay all of your cash gifts, he or she will reduce the amounts of each of those gifts on a *pro rata* basis, which means that they would all be reduced by the same percentage. The exact percentage would be calculated by dividing the total amount of cash gifts in your will by the actual amount of cash available in your probate estate.

Choosing an Executor

If your estate is large and complex, if you left it in disarray, and/or if there are any contests to your will, the probate process will be tedious, time-consuming and full of hassles for your executor. It will take more than a year—maybe a couple years to complete. However, if your probate estate is relatively small and simple, and no one contests your will, your executor should be able to complete the probate process relatively quickly—in less than a year—especially if your state has a streamlined probate process for very small estates and your estate qualifies for that process.

Generally speaking, given all of the things an executor is responsible for, you should choose as your executor someone who is organized, detail-oriented, good at meeting deadlines, and not easily overwhelmed by official forms and paperwork. Also, it's a good idea if your executor lives near you or has the flexibility to travel to your area as needed during the probate process.

It's also important that the person you choose meet all of your state's requirements for an executor. For example, every state requires that executors be legal adults and U.S. citizens, and most states also prohibit executors from being convicted felons. To find out if your state has any other requirements, talk with an estate planning attorney. If your executor does not meet all of your state's requirements, the probate judge will choose an executor for you. That person will be known as the *administrator* of your estate.

If you die without having designated an executor (and assuming that all of your assets are not transferring outside your will), the probate court will appoint an administrator for your estate. This person will be responsible for doing everything that your executor would do.

Should You Choose a Personal or a Professional Executor?

Most people designate their surviving spouse or partner, an adult child, sibling, or close friend as their executor (it is a good idea to designate at least one alternate executor, too). However, if you don't think that anyone you know would make a good executor, you can designate a professional, like your family attorney, banker, or CPA. If you opt for a professional, you may want to name a family member or a close friend as a coexecutor to help keep your family "in the loop" during the probate process. Designating a professional executor is a good decision if any of the following apply to your situation.

The value of your probate estate is substantial and includes complex assets. Complex assets include income-producing real estate or other income-producing assets, out-of-state assets, or business interests, especially if you own a business and you want it to continue operating after your death. Placing values on these kinds of assets, managing them during the probate process, and so on, requires special expertise that none of your relatives and friends may have.

You anticipate that some of your adult children or another one of your legal heirs may be unhappy with your will and may take out their anger on your executor. A professional executor is going to have an easier time dealing with such anger than a family member or close family friend probably will. Also, if your family members are prone to squabbles, and you are concerned that after you die they may fight over your will or disagree with the decisions your executor makes, you want an executor who can effectively resolve those problems out of court. A professional will have a better shot at doing that. Also, your family members will probably be less apt to ask the court to replace a professional executor if they are unhappy with something the executor has or hasn't done. If they do ask that your executor be replaced, the probate process will take longer and cost your estate more money.

You are worried that your will may be contested. A contest will take up a lot of your executor's time—maybe more time than a friend or family member would have bargained for. A professional executor will be more knowledgeable than an amateur about the rules of probate, will have staff to help him or her with all of the probate-related paperwork, and will be better prepared to deal with any problems that may arise.

However, keep in mind that a professional will also expect to be paid for his or her services. In contrast, most friends and family members who serve as executors usually waive the right to be paid. If you pay your executor, his or her fee will usually be a percentage—between two and five percent in most states—of the gross value of your probate estate (the value of all of the assets in your probate estate *before* debts, taxes, expenses, and fees have been paid). Before the executor fee can be paid, it must be approved by the probate court. The court may give your executor the right to charge an additional fee if probating your estate is unusually complicated and time-consuming.

Appointing Coexecutors

Rather than appointing one person to be your executor, you can designate coexecutors. If you do, be sure to choose two people who you think will work well together. A coexecutor arrangement might be a good alternative to a professional executor if you know two people who together embody all of the qualities you are looking for in an executor. For example, one of them has a good head for numbers and is great at filling out forms, and the other is a people person who will do a good job of dealing with your family, the probate attorney, the probate judge, and so on. Coexecutors can also make sense when your first choice for an executor lives out of state, and you want someone else close by to handle day-to-day probate matters.

A Few Other Executor Considerations

Most states require that executors be bonded. A bond is a financial guarantee that an executor will carry out all of his or her responsibilities without damaging your estate in any way or causing it to lose value. If your executor does harm your estate, the bonding company will reimburse your estate for the damage that's been done to it. However, if you don't want your executor to have to incur the cost of a bond, you can use your will to waive that obligation.

If you name a friend or family member as your executor, and he or she wants to receive a fee, you can minimize the likelihood that any of your family members will object to it during the probate process by spelling out exactly how much the fee will be and by providing a rationale in your will. Talk with an estate planning attorney about what would be fair in light of your estate, your family situation, and what your state allows. Then talk things over with the person you want to serve as your executor, and try to reach an agreement on the amount of the fee (if you don't waive the bonding requirement, you may want to include the amount of the bond in the fee). Once the two of you have come to an agreement, let your family members know what you've decided, and explain why you believe the fee is fair.

Before you ask someone to agree to be your executor, make sure that he or she understands exactly what the job will involve and believes that he or she will have the time to do it. Be honest about any possible problems you may foresee. Do the same with whomever you want to name as your alternate executor.

Proceeding through the Probate Process

The probate process helps ensure, among other things, that your creditors are paid in an orderly fashion, that any taxes your estate may owe are paid, and that the assets in your will are legally transferred to your beneficiaries according to the terms of your will.

The probate process will take place in the state in which you are legally residing at the time of your death, even if you wrote your will when you were living in another state. Ordinarily, as long as your will is legally valid in the state where you wrote it, its validity won't be an issue. However, if there are questions about any aspects of your will or any will contests, the probate court in your last state of residence will resolve those issues according to its own laws, which may be quite different from the laws of the state in which you resided when you wrote the will. Also, if you own real property in the state where you used to live, those assets will be probated there. This means that your executor will have to deal with two different probate courts, unless you named an *ancillary executor* in your will—someone who lives in that other state. If you didn't, your executor probably will hire a probate attorney in that other state to help him or her (in addition to the attorney your executor probably hired to help with the probate process in the state where you died). Your estate will pay the costs of that legal help.

The cost of probating your will and the amount of time it will take to complete the probate process will depend on many factors including:

- Whether or not your executor, or someone else, knows where your will is located.
- Whether there is any question about the legal validity of your will.
- Whether you left your financial affairs in good order.
- The size and complexity of your estate.
- Whether there are any contests.
- The organizational skills and efficiency of your executor.
- The general nature of the probate process in the state(s) where your will is being probated; the process in some states moves along much more quickly than in others.

The assets in your will cannot be distributed to your beneficiaries until the probate process is nearly over, and the longer it takes to complete that process, the greater the likelihood that your family's finances will be strained. This is especially true if you were the sole or primary breadwinner and your family doesn't have access to cash from some other source, like the proceeds from a life insurance policy or the funds in your retirement accounts. However, your state may have a family allowance law, which will provide your family with a limited amount of money to help pay their living expenses during the probate process. The amount of the allowance varies by state. It may be based on the size of your family, the amount of your family's living expenses, and/or on the value of your estate.

This chapter explained the purpose of the probate process and how it relates to your will. Before the assets in your will can be distributed to your beneficiaries after your death, they must go through the state court–supervised process called probate. The person you designate in your will as your executor will guide your estate through that process. It also explained the specific responsibilities that your executor must carry out during the probate process, highlighted issues to consider when you are deciding who to name as your executor, discussed the pros and cons of designating a friend or relative versus a financial professional, a bank trust department, or a trust company, and described when a coexecutor arrangement may be appropriate. This chapter gave an overview of the various factors that will influence the cost of probating your estate and the amount of time it takes to complete the process.

The Lowdown on Living Trusts

oth a living trust and a will accomplish the same basic estate planning goal—they each provide you with a means of transferring your assets to your beneficiaries when you die. However, a living trust and a will work very differently, and you can do things with a living trust that you can't do with a will.

Living Trust Basics

A trust is a legal entity that exists to hold assets for the benefit of one or more beneficiaries. Think of it as a cookie jar for your assets. A living trust, which is sometimes referred to as an inter vivos trust, is a special kind of trust that you create while you are alive by preparing a signed trust agreement. Unlike a testamentary trust, which was discussed in Chapter 4, a living trust is *not* a part of your will.

Although the specific requirements for a trust agreement vary somewhat from state to state, in general your agreement will spell out all of the details of the trust. This includes the name(s) of your trust beneficiary(ies), the name of the trustee—the person who will manage the trust—the powers that you are giving to the trustee,

Funding your living trust involves taking ownership of your assets out of your name and putting ownership into the name of the trust.

what the assets in the trust can be used for and what can be done with any income they may generate, any special terms and conditions that apply to the trust, when the trust will end, and what will happen to the trust assets when that happens. In addition, your trust agreement will either include a list of all of the assets that you are transferring to the trust or a separate attachment that itemizes all of the assets and provides the specific schedule of when they will be transferred.

When you prepare a trust agreement, you are formally referred to as a *grantor, settlor, trustor,* or *donor,* depending on the state in which you reside, and the trust assets are referred to as the trust *principal* or *corpus.* Also, the process of transferring those assets to the trust is described as *funding* the trust.

Funding your living trust involves taking ownership of your assets out of your name and putting ownership into the name of the trust. Depending on the kinds of assets you put in the trust, this may involve changing the name on the deeds to your real estate and on the titles to your vehicles, filling out new account applications for your bank and brokerage accounts, and so on.

Even though the trust becomes the legal owner of your assets, you can still control them and benefit from them just as you do now, by designating yourself as both trustee and beneficiary of the trust. If you are married or living with a partner and you set up a joint trust, you will probably act as cotrustees, and both of you will benefit from the trust. You can also opt not to manage your own trust and let someone else manage it on your behalf according to the instructions you set out in your trust agreement. That someone might be a close relative or friend, one of your financial advisors, the trust department of your bank, or a trust company.

No matter whom you designate as the trustee of your living trust, be sure to name at least one successor trustee. This person will manage your trust if your first choice for trustee dies, becomes too ill or injured to manage it, or decides that he or she doesn't want to mange it anymore. If you're setting up your spouse or partner as the trustee, he or she should also designate a successor trustee.

Depending on the purpose of a living trust, you may designate someone other than yourself to benefit from it, and you can also designate more than one beneficiary. Your trust beneficiary(ies) might be your spouse or partner, children, siblings, pets, favorite charities, alma mater, church, and so on.

A living trust can be revocable or irrevocable, but if you're making a living trust the foundation of your estate plan, it should be a revocable trust. That way, while you are alive and mentally competent, you can change anything and everything about the trust in response to changes in your life. In fact, in the world of estate planning, the terms *living trust* and *revocable living trust* are virtually interchangeable. Throughout this book, unless otherwise indicated, the term *living trust* refers to a revocable living trust.

Usually, *irrevocable trusts* are used to accomplish one or more very specific estate planning goals. For example, an irrevocable trust can be set up to minimize your estate taxes, to provide for your disabled child, to control what your adult children can do with the assets that you are leaving to them, or to prevent a financially irresponsible beneficiary from squandering the assets you want him or her to benefit from. An irrevocable trust can let your surviving spouse or partner benefit from your estate after your death and ensure at the same time that your assets will go to the children from your first marriage after he or she dies. Depending on the purpose of your irrevocable living trust, you may have it set up and funded while you are alive and well, upon your incapacitation, or after your death.

Usually, irrevocable trusts are used to accomplish one or more very specific estate planning goals.

**Compared to
a will, a living
trust has some
attractive
advantages.**

Advantages of a Living Trust

Compared to a will, a living trust has some attractive advantages. The following are some of the advantages of preparing a living trust.

It avoids probate. This is one of the primary reasons why many people build their estate plans on a living trust. Because none of the assets in your living trust will go through the probate process, your trust beneficiaries will benefit from them sooner—maybe as quickly as a couple of weeks or months after you die, depending on the number of assets in your trust and their complexity. Also, the value of your estate won't be diminished by all of the legal fees and other expenses associated with probate, which means that there will be more of your estate to benefit your beneficiaries.

Bear in mind, however, that many of your assets may avoid probate without having to be transferred to a living trust. For example, property owned jointly with the right of survivorship, as well as retirement assets and life insurance with designated beneficiaries, don't go through probate.

There may be other reasons why avoiding probate is important to you. For example, you'll keep the details of your estate plan out of the public record, which may be especially important to you if you are disinheriting one of your children, providing for a child with a substance abuse problem, or doing something else with your estate plan that you'd prefer to keep private. Also, in the midst of their grief, your loved ones won't have to deal with court paperwork, procedures, and red tape.

It can provide for you and your loved ones if you become incapacitated. You can word your living trust agreement so that if you can no longer manage the trust because of a serious illness or injury, your successor trustee (or cotrustee) can automatically begin managing it for you. No probate court proceeding will be required to make that happen, and everything about your trust will continue to be private.

In contrast, if you become incapacitated and you've built your estate plan on a will, the probate court will have to formally appoint your financial agent—the person you appointed in your durable power of attorney document to manage your finances when you are too ill or injured to do it yourself. Also, the court will monitor your agent's actions by requiring that he or she provide it with regular reports about your finances, all of which will be part of the public record. If you write a will but you don't legally designate your financial agent, the probate court will appoint one for you through a public process.

It can hold out-of-state property, like real estate. If you transfer all of your out-of-state assets to a living trust while you are alive, you won't incur the costs and delays associated with probate in other states.

You can control when your beneficiaries will actually receive their inheritances. You can opt for your beneficiaries to take control of their inheritances right away, over time, or down the road. Your trust agreement can also allow them to benefit from the trust but never give them access to the trust assets. With a will, however, once the probate process is over, your beneficiaries will receive whatever you've left to them. If you've left any of your assets directly to your minor children, they will get control of them as soon as they become legal adults—no matter how much those assets may be worth and regardless of the fact that most 18 and 21 year olds

You can opt for your beneficiaries to take control of their inheritances right away, over time, or down the road.

don't have the knowledge or experience to be good financial managers. However, you can control when your beneficiaries will receive their inheritances after you die if their assets are transferred to a testamentary trust through your will.

You'll incur most of the estate planning costs while you are alive. Because your living trust will be set up and funded while you are alive, it will be easier for you to control your estate planning costs and to plan how you will pay them. In contrast, if you build your estate plan on a will, most of your estate planning costs won't be incurred until after your death. Therefore, it will be difficult while you are alive to get a firm fix on how much those costs will amount to, which means that it will be difficult for you to minimize them and plan for how to pay them.

It's more difficult to contest. Though it's possible for one of your disgruntled heirs to contest your living trust, living trusts are a lot harder to contest than wills. Also, living trust contests tend to be less successful and, while a contest is being resolved, the assets in living trusts are frozen. This is unlike what usually happens when a will is contested.

It makes things easier for your family after your death. Funding a living trust forces you to pull together all of your ownership paperwork now, before you become incapacitated or die, and if there are any problems with any of those documents, you and your attorney can resolve them. If you build your estate on a will, however, you'll probably leave all of the document gathering to your executor and your family. If there are any problems, the probate process will take longer and cost more.

The Disadvantages of a Living Trust

Despite their many advantages, living trusts have some disadvantages, too. The following are some of the disadvantages of preparing a living trust.

Setting up a living trust tends to be more complicated and time-consuming than preparing a will. This is mainly because of the time it takes to transfer ownership of the assets out of your name and into the name of the trust. However, if you work with an estate planning attorney, he or she should handle all of the transfer paperwork for you.

You'll have to pay your attorney an additional fee each time you want to amend your living trust. This fee is a small price to pay to ensure that whatever changes you make are handled correctly. Furthermore, if you build your estate plan on a will and you are working with an estate planning attorney, you'll have to pay him or her extra money whenever you want to amend your will.

You may have to pay a transfer tax when you transfer real estate to your living trust. Whether you will owe a tax depends on your state. The government office in your county that maintains property deed records can tell you if your state imposes such a tax and the amount of the tax. If you work with an estate planning attorney, he or she will know.

It may be a little more difficult to refinance a mortgage on property that is in your living trust. However, you can resolve this problem simply by providing the lender with a copy of your living trust agreement. If that doesn't work, you can always transfer the real estate out of the trust, refinance it, and then transfer it back into the trust. Doing so may be a bit of a hassle, but it would get the job done.

You may have trouble getting auto insurance for a vehicle that is in a living trust because you won't own the car. Again, providing the insurance company with a copy of your trust agreement will probably do the trick.

It doesn't eliminate the need for a will. You'll still need a will in order to transfer any assets you may have forgotten about into your living trust after your death. You'll also need a will to transfer any assets you received just prior to your death, such as an inheritance. A will that serves this function is referred to as a *pour-over will.* Also, if you are the parent of minor children, you need a will to legally designate their personal guardian—the adult you want to raise them should you and their other parent both die before they become legal adults.

While you are alive, the assets in your living trust won't be protected from your creditors. Your creditors can put liens on your trust assets, repossess them, and foreclose on them, just like they could before the assets were in the trust (an irrevocable trust *does* shield assets from creditors, however). Also, in most states, after your death your creditors will have more time to try to collect from the assets in your living trust than they would if you had transferred them through a will.

Your divorce will have no effect on your living trust. If you get divorced after you've set up a living trust, the trust agreement won't be revoked automatically, nor will the specific provisions that relate to your ex be cancelled automatically. That means that if you don't amend the terms of your living trust after your divorce, your former spouse could end up inheriting your assets when you die. If you build your estate plan on a will, however, once your divorce is final, the court will automatically revoke your entire will or cancel the provisions that apply to your ex.

Is a Living Trust Right for You?

Whether you should build your estate plan on a living trust or on a will is going to depend on how you weigh their individual advantages versus their individual disadvantages. Generally, however, a living trust doesn't make sense when:

- You don't own many assets. This is especially true if your assets are worth little and your state has established a streamlined, lower-cost probate process for small estates that your estate can use.
- The assets you own are uncomplicated, so managing them doesn't require any special knowledge or skills.
- Most of your assets won't have to be probated.
- You believe that it's unlikely that any of your legal heirs will contest the terms of your estate plan.
- At your death, most of what you own will be transferred through joint tenancy ownership, inter vivos gifts, custodial accounts, your retirement accounts, and so on.
- You don't care that the probate court will be involved in your life and the lives of your family members if you die or become incapacitated, and you've built your estate on a will. However, this is becoming an issue for many people, especially individuals in their fifties and sixties—many of whom can expect to live well into their eighties, nineties, or even beyond.

Whether you should build your estate plan on a living trust or on a will is going to depend on how you weigh their individual advantages versus their individual disadvantages.

If you decide to build your estate plan on a living trust, you will have many important decisions to make when you are preparing your trust agreement.

■ Maintaining your privacy isn't important to you.

If you decide that right now a living trust is not for you, you may opt for one later because you've acquired many more assets or your family situation has become a lot more complicated. Or maybe you've developed a debilitating illness that you anticipate will eventually make it impossible for you to manage your own finances, and you don't want the court involved in your life when that happens, and so on.

Key Decisions When You Set Up a Living Trust

If you decide to build your estate plan on a living trust, you will have many important decisions to make when you are preparing your trust agreement. Your estate planning attorney will help you make those decisions, taking into account your finances, your family relationships, and other issues that may be important to you. The following are some of the basic decisions you will have to make.

Will Your Trust Be an Individual or a Joint Trust?

If you are single, you will probably have an individual trust, although you can set up a joint trust with someone else, such as your partner. If you are married, you and your spouse will probably set up a joint trust, which will hold all of your joint assets as well as all of your individual assets, because it will be easier to manage your finances if everything is in one trust. This is particularly true if you live in a community property state where each of you owns one-half of your marital assets. Having only half of those assets in the trust will be needlessly compli-cated (Chapter 2 explains how property ownership for married couples works in community property states). If you are married it's also possible for you to set up an individual trust that holds your separate property and a joint trust that holds the assets you and your spouse own together. However, most married couples just opt for a joint trust.

Putting your individual assets into a joint trust won't change their nature—they'll still be your very own assets. Therefore, while they are in the trust, it will be your decision and no one else's if you want to borrow against them, sell them, or transfer them out of the trust. Also, you and you alone will decide what should happen to those assets if you become incapacitated or when you die.

Who Will Manage the Trust While You're Alive?

If you are like most people with an individual living trust, you'll act as your own trustee. If you have a joint trust that you've set up with your spouse or partner, the two of you will act as cotrustees, managing the trust assets together. However, you also have the option of not being the trustee (or cotrustee) of your living trust. You may make that choice because you are in poor health, you're not a good money manager, or you simply don't want the responsibility. Even so, if someone else manages your living trust, you'll still control the trust assets through the instructions in your trust agreement, and you can "fire" your trustee if you are unhappy with him or her and name a new one.

Who Will Manage the Trust if You Become Incapacitated?

If your trust is an individual living trust and you are the trustee, whomever you name as your successor trustee will manage the trust on your behalf if you become incapacitated. Your successor trustee might be your spouse, your partner, a close friend, a sibling, or someone else. If you're not the trustee, then your incapacitation will have no affect on the trust management.

If you and your spouse or partner are cotrustees of a joint trust, depending on the terms of the trust, your spouse or partner may manage it by himself or herself, which is what usually happens. Your successor trustee will manage the trust alone, or your successor trustee and your spouse will manage it together as cotrustees. Factors that might influence your decision about what should happen may include: your spouse's financial management abilities, the types of assets that are in the trust and whether your spouse has the particular expertise that is needed to mange them, the health of your spouse, and your spouse's own wishes, among other things.

Who Will Manage the Trust When You Die?

If you've set up an individual trust, your successor trustee will handle all of the tasks necessary for the trust assets to be distributed to your beneficiaries in accordance with the instructions you set out in your trust agreement. Those tasks will include paying your outstanding debts, including any taxes your estate may owe; working with your brokerage firm, mortgage company, bank, and so on to transfer your assets to your living trust beneficiaries; and distributing any trust assets that don't have ownership paperwork, like jewelry, collectibles, antique furniture, and so on, to the appropriate beneficiaries. Once all of your assets have been transferred out of the trust, the trust will end.

If you and your spouse are cotrustees of a joint living trust, after your death the trust will become an individual trust, which will include any assets you want your spouse to benefit from, as well as your spouse's own assets. Your spouse will probably manage the trust on behalf of your family, including any minor children the two of you may have together, and your spouse may also have the right to determine what will happen to all of the trust assets when he or she dies. However, depending on your estate planning goals, the trust instructions may require that some of your assets be distributed directly to certain beneficiaries. Or the instructions may specify that some of your assets be transferred out of your joint living trust into one or more new trusts, like a trust for your children or a trust to minimize estate taxes. All of the terms and conditions of these other trusts will be spelled out in your trust agreement.

Some people designate two successor trustees in their living trust agreement—one to manage their living trust if they become incapacitated and another to manage it after their death. The rationale is that the skills and personal characteristics needed to manage a trust in one situation are quite different from what may be needed in the other.

What Assets Will You Put in Your Trust?

You will probably transfer all of your assets to your living trust, including your bank accounts, money market accounts, certificates of deposit, publicly traded stocks, bonds, mutual funds and other securities, real estate, and life insurance policies—with the exception of your tax-deferred retirement assets, like your individual retirement account or IRA (but not a Roth IRA) and your 401(k). The reason you shouldn't put your tax-deferred retirement assets in the trust is that when you transfer those assets out of your name and into the name of the trust, the transfers will be treated like withdrawals. As a result, you will owe income taxes on them because you

It goes without saying that whomever you choose as your successor trustee should be someone you completely trust.

didn't pay any taxes on your income when you made deposits into those accounts.

Who Will Be the Beneficiaries of Your Living Trust When You Die?

Your beneficiaries may include your spouse or partner if you set up an individual trust, your children, other relatives, your friends, your alma mater, your pets, your favorite charity, and so on. You can direct that the assets you want them to benefit from be distributed directly to your beneficiaries, or that they be transferred into one or more trusts for your beneficiaries. The "Special Trusts for Special Purposes" section of this chapter highlights some of the kinds of trusts that are commonly set up through a living trust. It also discusses some of the more common irrevocable trusts that you might set up in addition to your living trust, in order to help you achieve a specific estate planning goal.

Selecting a Successor Trustee

It goes without saying that whomever you choose as your successor trustee should be someone you completely trust. However, in the interests of good trust management, your successor should also:

- **Be able to get along with your spouse or partner** if the two of them will be cotrustees.
- **Have the time to mange your trust.** Trust management can be time-consuming, depending on the number of assets in a trust, their value, and their complexity.
- **Have the financial management knowledge and skills** needed to manage the trust assets. For example, if your trust includes a lot of investment real estate, then you would not want to choose a real estate neophyte as your successor trustee.

- **Be willing to take on the job of managing your trust.** Never name someone as your successor trustee unless you are sure that he or she understands what managing your trust will take and is willing to do the job.
- **Be familiar with your values and attitudes.** Although these are not essential qualities in a successor trustee, having an intimate understanding of who you are and what makes you tick can be helpful. For example, it could help in the event that your trust agreement contains something that is ambiguous or if an issue arises that your trust agreement does not explicitly address. If your successor trustee knows you well, he or she can use that information as a context for deciding what you were trying to convey in the agreement and/or what you would do under the circumstances.

Personal or Professional Trust Management?

Most people choose a close relative or friend as their successor trustee. However, if no one you know is right for the job, you may want to consider designating a bank trust department or a trust company, especially if your trust assets are worth a substantial amount of money and/or if managing them requires special expertise. For example, your trust may include business interests, investments, a large stock portfolio, and so on. A bank trust department or a trust company will have all of the systems and resources necessary to do a professional job of managing all these details of your trust in accordance with your wishes. Also, given that they are in the trust management business, they will be less apt to make mistakes that might harm the integrity and value of your trust to the detriment of your trust beneficiaries.

Professional trust management is also a good idea if the beneficiaries of your trust do not get along and

Cost is the biggest drawback associated with professional trust management.

you want a trustee who will be relatively removed from their conflicts. If one of your relatives or friends is the trustee, he or she is more apt to be drawn into your family's dramas and as a result, those dramas might influence how he or she manages the trust.

Cost is the biggest drawback associated with professional trust management. Though anyone who acts as your successor trustee is legally entitled to receive a "reasonable fee," which will be paid by your trust, family members and friends often waive their right to receive a fee. However a bank trust department or a trust company will expect to be paid, and what they charge will be substantially more than what a friend or family member would charge if he or she wanted to be paid. Even so, if you have a very large estate and you want to make certain that your living trust is managed well, you may decide that putting a bank trust department or a trust company in charge of your trust is worth the price.

If you choose a friend or family member as your successor trustee and he or she waives the right to a fee, it's a good idea to include a provision in your trust agreement that entitles your friend or relative to a fair fee anyway, especially if managing your trust will be a time-consuming job or if the trust is likely to exist for many years. Otherwise, your friend or relative may begin to resent the amount of time it takes to manage the trust and as a result, he or she may begin neglecting it. If that happens, the trust assets might lose value and the beneficiaries of your trust, including you if you are incapacitated, might be harmed.

Special Trusts for Special Purposes

Your living trust instructions may direct that upon your death or incapacitation, new trusts with special purposes should be set up and funded. This section describes some of the kinds of trusts that are most often set up through a living trust (Chapter 8 tells you more about some of them). You can create these same kinds of trusts through your will when you die, but the assets you want transferred to the trusts will go through probate first, so they won't be available to the trust beneficiaries as quickly as if you set up one or more living trusts.

By the way, some kinds of trusts have more than one name. To eliminate some of the confusion, the most common names are listed here. Furthermore, the best rule of thumb when you are reading about a trust is to focus on what it does rather than on what it's called.

A/B Trust

This kind of trust is the most common kind of tax-saving trust. It allows both spouses to use their individual federal estate tax exemptions to maximize the amount of assets that they can pass on to their beneficiaries, usually their children, tax-free. An A/B trust is actually two trusts—a revocable A trust, also called a *marital trust* or *survivor's trust,* and an irrevocable B trust, also known as a *bypass trust, credit shelter trust, decedent's trust,* or *family trust.* Like all tax-saving trusts, an A/B trust must be set up in accordance with IRS rules and must include very precise wording. If it doesn't, it might not achieve its goals.

Trusts for Your Children

You can use your living trust to set up, after your death, an irrevocable common trust for the benefit all of your minor or adult children or an individual trusts for each of them. Chapter 9 covers living trust and children in more detail.

Special Needs Trust

You should consider this kind of irrevocable trust if you want to give a share of your estate to someone with a serious disability and you want to be sure that the value of the assets won't jeopardize his or her eligibility for important government benefits like Medicaid and Supplemental Security Income (SSI). SSI is a federal program that helps disabled people of limited financial means pay for their basic living expenses, like food, clothing, and housing. Medicaid is a federal and state program that provides people of limited means with health care services. Both of these benefits are only available to individuals who own very few assets and have very low incomes.

With a special needs trust, your beneficiary will have no control over the trust assets and therefore, those assets will not be counted when his or her eligibility for governmental assistance is being determined. Special needs trusts are commonly used to pay for the things that government programs don't cover, such as vacations, furniture, other household items, education, vehicles, out-of-pocket medical expenses, personal care attendants, and so on.

Spendthrift Trust

This kind of irrevocable trust is set up to benefit someone—you guessed it—who is a spendthrift. In other words, someone who is likely to mismanage and squander his or her inheritance if it's paid directly to him or her. This kind of trust is also appropriate for someone with an addiction. The beneficiary of a spendthrift trust has no access to the trust assets or income; instead, the trustee doles out money to the beneficiary and pays his or her bills. In addition, the beneficiary's creditors cannot come after the trust assets in order to collect from him or her, with two exceptions: past-due child and spousal support. However, creditors can try to collect from any income the beneficiary may have already received from the trust.

Qualified Terminable Interest Property (QTIP) Trust

A QTIP trust, which is an irrevocable trust, lets you take care of your surviving spouse or partner after your death and at the same time control what will happen to the remaining trust assets after he or she dies. It's a good option if you have children from a previous marriage and you want to make certain, after the death of your surviving spouse or partner, that all of the trust assets will go to them. Without a QTIP trust, your spouse might spend all of the assets, lose some of them to his or her creditors, leave them to his or her own children from a prior marriage, or get married and pass the assets on to his or her new spouse.

Irrevocable Life Insurance Trust

This kind of trust gets set up and funded while you are alive because its main purpose is to reduce the amount of your estate taxes. You do that by transferring your life insurance policy(ies) out of your name and into the name of the trust so that you no longer own them. If you die within three years of transferring the policy to the trust, however, the policy's value will be included in your taxable estate. Once the policy is in the trust, you cannot borrow against it or change the policy beneficiaries. However, through the trust agreement, you can control what the policy proceeds may be used for after your death.

Charitable Trusts

Charitable trusts let you benefit charities, as well as non-charities, while you are alive or after your death. These irrevocable trusts can also help you reduce the value of your taxable estate. The two most common types of charitable trusts are:

1. **Charitable lead trust (CLT).** This kind of trust provides a certain amount of income for a specific period of time to the charity(ies) that you've designated in your trust agreement. When that time is up, the trust assets and income benefit the noncharity beneficiary(ies) named in your trust agreement. Normally, you will transfer highly appreciated investment property to a CLT so that you can benefit from the profits without having to pay a capital gains tax. A capital gains tax is a tax on the profit you would make if you sold the investments.

2. **Charitable remainder trust (CRT).** This kind of trust benefits your designated noncharity beneficiary(ies) first and then your charity beneficiary(ies).

Educational Trust

This kind of trust has one purpose and one purpose only—to pay for someone else's education. You can set up an education trust to benefit one student or multiple students, perhaps all of your children or grandchildren, for example. The trust makes payments directly to the beneficiary(ies), which may be used to pay for books, educational supplies, fees, and tuition.

Generation-Skipping Trust

Assuming this kind of irrevocable trust is set up exactly right, you can transfer substantial amounts of your estate to your grandchildren or to other members of your family who are at least two generations junior to you, free of estate taxes.

Grantor Retained Trusts

These irrevocable trusts allow you to reduce your future tax liability and receive a steady stream of income from the trust assets, either for the rest of your life or for another period specified in your trust agreement. Income-producing assets like real estate, stocks, or a family business are often transferred to grantor retained trusts, which include a *grantor retained annuity trust,* a *grantor retained interest trust,* and a *qualified personal residence trust.* Here is an overview of how these three types of trusts work:

1. Grantor retained annuity trust (GRAT). This kind of trust pays you a set amount of money each year (an annuity). When you die, the trust assets go to your designated beneficiary(ies).
2. Grantor retained income trust (GRIT). The payments you receive during the term of this kind of trust will vary depending on the value of the trust assets.
3. Qualified personal residence trust (QPRT). When you set up this kind of trust, you remove your home from your taxable estate, but you continue to live in it for a predetermined length of time, usually 10 to 15 years. Then ownership of your house is either transferred directly to your beneficiary(ies), usually your children, or to another trust.

Legal Assistance Required

Living trusts can be very complicated, and if they're not set up exactly right, they won't do what you want them

Living trusts can be very complicated, and if they're not set up exactly right, they won't do what you want them to do.

to do. Therefore, it's never a good idea to try to set up your own living trust. Always work with an estate planning attorney who has living trust experience.

Purchasing a living trust at an estate planning/living trust seminar or from someone who is selling living trusts—even from an attorney selling them—is also a bad idea. All you'll get for your money is a one-size-fits-all living trust and nothing more—no help funding the trust, none of the other legal documents that belong in your estate plan, like a pour-over will and a durable medical power of attorney, and no periodic reviews and meetings to determine whether your trust needs updating or whether you need to amend any other part of your estate plan.

Another important reason to work with an estate planning attorney is that your living trust should be coordinated with the rest of your estate plan so that all of the pieces of your plan work together as a cohesive whole. An estate planning attorney will help you do that. For example, your attorney will:

- Prepare your pour-over will and make sure, if you have minor children, that you designate a personal guardian for them in your will.
- Make sure that your successor trustee has the right to pay any taxes your estate may owe when you die and the right to pay any probate-related expenses your estate may owe if some of your assets end up going through that process.
- Help you figure out how any estate taxes your estate may owe when you die will be paid.
- Make sure that your estate plan includes the appropriate advance medical directives, as well as a durable power of attorney for your finances.

- Ensure that you have all of the appropriate insurance, which may include disability insurance, health insurance, life insurance, long-term care insurance, and so on.
- Coordinate your retirement accounts with the rest of your estate plan.

Bottom line: Setting up your own trust is a bad idea. In the end, you and your beneficiaries may pay the price for your misguided penny-pinching.

This chapter discussed the advantages and the disadvantages of building your estate plan on a living trust rather than a will. It helped you understand whether a living trust–based estate plan is something you may want to consider, given the size and complexity of your estate, your family situation, and your estate planning goals. You should now be more aware of the kinds of decisions you will have to make if you set up a living trust, as well as some of the kinds of specialized trusts you may want to create through your living trust. This includes trusts to provide for your children, for a mentally or physically disabled dependent, for someone with a spending problem, to benefit your favorite charity, and to save on estate taxes. In addition, the information provided regarding the complexity of living trusts and the importance of hiring an estate planning attorney should help you make key decisions regarding your estate planning needs.

Estate Planning Beyond Your Will

Chapter 7

hen you purchased your life insurance policy, set up your IRA, or established a regular or a Roth 401(k) account through your employer and designated a beneficiary for each, you probably didn't realize that you were doing estate planning—but you were. In fact, life insurance, retirement accounts, payable-on-death accounts, and custodial accounts are commonly referred to as *will substitutes*. That's because they provide a means of transferring assets to designated beneficiaries outside of your will, which means that, with a few exceptions, those assets won't go through the probate process when you die, so they will be readily available to whomever you've left them to. Living trusts and inter vivos gifts (assets that you give away while you are alive) are also will substitutes, as are joint tenancy assets.

By and large, these will substitutes are a quick and easy way to transfer assets. However, there are some important drawbacks associated with most types of will substitutes. For example, with the exception of a living trust, when you transfer an asset via a will substitute, you don't get to control when the beneficiary of that asset can have access to it or what he or she can use the asset

It doesn't matter if you left your home to someone else in your will because when it comes to joint tenancy assets, title rules.

for. Instead, assuming your will substitute beneficiary is a legal adult when you die or when you give him or her an inter vivos gift, the asset will pass directly to your beneficiary with no strings attached. Although this may not be a problem if the value of the asset is rather small, it could be disastrous if your beneficiary is young and immature, is financially uninformed, has an addiction, has a manipulative and greedy spouse or partner, and so on.

Estate Planning with Joint Tenancy Assets

When an asset is titled as a joint tenancy asset, you and one or more co-owners each own an equal share of the asset. When one of you dies, that owner's interest in the asset automatically transfers to the surviving co-owners. For example, if you and your spouse own your home as joint tenants and you die first, your spouse ends up owning the entire house. If you own the house with multiple co-owners and you die first, then your share automatically transfers in equal amounts to each of your surviving co-owners. It doesn't matter if you left your home to someone else in your will because when it comes to joint tenancy assets, title rules.

The same is true for assets that you may own with your spouse as tenants by the entirety. As discussed in Chapter 2, this form of joint ownership is only available to spouses and only in some states. Joint tenancy assets work differently in community property states, and Chapter 2 explains why.

Before you run out and make all of your assets joint tenancy assets, however, consider the disadvantages of this kind of ownership:

- **While you're alive, you won't have full control** over your joint tenancy assets. For example, although you can sell your share of a joint tenancy asset, you cannot sell the entire asset unless all of the co-owners agree to the sale.

- **You could end up owning a joint tenancy asset with someone you do not know** or may not get along with if one of your co-owners sells his or her share or loses the asset in a divorce.

- **Your joint tenancy assets will be subject to the liabilities** of each of your co-owners. For example, if one of your co-owners owes a past due debt or owes a money judgment to someone as a result of a lawsuit, the creditor or whoever got the judgment may try to collect his or her money by going after one of your joint tenancy assets. The fact that you may have forked over most of the money for the asset won't matter. How the asset is titled is what matters.

- **If one of your co-owners becomes physically or mentally incapacitated** and didn't plan ahead of time for that eventuality, you'll have to get approval from the probate court to borrow against the asset, refinance a loan that's secured by the asset, or sell the asset. Getting that approval could take time, and the delay could cause your estate to lose value.

- **You won't have the right to determine who will get your share** of a joint tenancy asset when you die unless you outlive your co-owners and end up owning all of the asset yourself. If you die first, how the asset is titled determines who gets your share. Here's an example of why this could be a problem. Let's assume that 15 years ago, you and your sister inherited your parent's beach house and that the two of you own it as joint tenants. In addition, you and your sister have an understanding that whoever lives the longest will transfer their share of the house to the other's children, so that they can share it with their own children. Let's also assume that you die first, so now your sister owns 100 percent of the house. Here's the problem: Nothing prevents your sister from falling in love after you die, getting married, revising her will to reflect her change in marital status, and leaving the beach house to her spouse, not to your kids.

■ **Your joint tenancy assets could have negative tax consequences** for you and your co-owners, and there may be nothing you can do while you are alive to avoid them. For example, your co-owners could owe federal estate taxes as a result of ending up with your share of a joint tenancy asset. You could decide to retitle one of your individual assets as a joint tenancy asset in order to give part of your ownership interest to someone else as an inter vivos gift. If the value of the share that you give away is greater than the amount of your annual gift tax exclusion, which was $12,000 at the time this book was printed, you will reduce the total amount of your lifetime federal estate tax exemption and, as a result, your estate could end up owing federal estate taxes when you die. (Chapter 2 discusses federal estate taxes and how your lifetime federal estate tax exemption works.) Furthermore, if the person to whom you've given the inter vivos gift outlives you and decides to sell the asset after your death, he or she will have to pay a capital gains tax on any profit realized from the sale. That would not be the case if you had transferred the asset to him or her through your will or through a living trust.

Life Insurance

When you own a life insurance policy, your life insurance company pays the beneficiary of the policy a death benefit when you die. Most married people make their spouse their beneficiary, but you may decide to designate your children, your unmarried partner, a close friend, someone else who is financially dependent on you, a charity, or a trust as your policy beneficiary. It's your decision. You may also purchase multiple life insurance policies and name a different beneficiary for each policy. Whatever you do, don't forget to designate at least one alternate beneficiary for each of your beneficiaries. If your first choice for a beneficiary is already deceased when you die or dies before the proceeds can be distributed, your state will determine who will end up with the policy proceeds according to its intestacy law.

You may decide to purchase one or more life insurance policies for many reasons, including the following.

- You may wish to increase the size of your estate so that your loved ones will end up with more money when you die.
- After your death, the policy death benefit can be used to pay the costs of probate, as well as any debts and/or estate taxes your estate may owe. Without that money, some of your assets—assets that would otherwise go to the beneficiaries of your will or to your legal heirs if you die without a will—will have to be sold to pay those obligations.
- Your surviving spouse or partner can use the policy death benefit to pay for your cremation or burial.
- The death benefit can provide your family with the money needed to cover their living expenses while the probate process is taking place.

Whenever you purchase life insurance, review your policy periodically to make certain that the amount of

Whatever you do, don't forget to designate at least one alternate beneficiary for each of your beneficiaries.

the policy is adequate and that you don't want to change your beneficiary(ies). If you decide that you want to amend your policy, call the insurance agent who sold it to you. The agent will send you a form to fill out and return.

Unraveling the Differences between Term, Whole Life, and Universal Insurance

The three basic types of life insurance are *term life insurance, whole life insurance,* and *universal life insurance.* Each type is outlined below.

Term life insurance. Term life insurance is the least expensive kind of insurance because it's pure insurance. In other words, when you purchase term life insurance all you get is a policy that covers you for a fixed time—the term—and that pays a death benefit to your beneficiary.

Whole life insurance. Whole life insurance is insurance that remains in effect as long as you continue to pay your policy premiums and it includes a savings feature. When you purchase this kind of insurance, a portion of each of your monthly payments goes to fund your policy's death benefit, and another portion goes into a tax-deferred savings account. The savings portion represents the cash value of your policy. While you are alive, you can borrow against that cash value and you can repay the loan according to whatever schedule works for you. You can also opt not to repay the loan or just to repay part of it. However, if any of the loan is still outstanding when you die, your insurance company will deduct the amount of the outstanding balance from the total amount of your policy death benefit, which means that your beneficiary will end up with less money than if you had repaid the loan.

Universal life insurance. Universal life insurance is a type of whole life, cash value insurance that features, among other things, flexible premiums and adjustable death benefits.

A Word of Caution

If you are going to purchase a relatively large life insurance policy, it's a good idea to discuss your plans with an estate planning attorney, especially if you own a substantial amount of other assets. This is because without the appropriate up-front planning, the policy could have negative, unintended consequences for you or your policy beneficiary(ies). For example:

■ If you make your estate the beneficiary of the policy, when you die the death benefits will be included in your probate estate. In other words, they will not transfer outside of your will. The same is true if you own the policy at the time of your death. As a result, among other problems, the policy death benefits will go through the probate process, which means that they will not be immediately available. Also, the value of your policy will increase your estate's probate costs, and it may also increase the amount of federal estate taxes your estate may owe. With the right planning, however, you can avoid these problems. For example, you can transfer the policy to your spouse or someone else—maybe to an irrevocable life insurance trust—so that the policy proceeds are no longer in your estate. However, the transfer must occur at least three years prior to your death.

- The amount of the policy death benefit could create a future estate tax problem for your beneficiary, depending on how much the rest of his or her estate is worth.

- You can't place any limits or conditions on when your policy beneficiary will receive the policy proceeds or what he or she can do with them. One way to get around this problem is to make a living trust your policy beneficiary.

- If you make a minor child your policy beneficiary, the child's property guardian will manage the policy proceeds subject to all of the probate court's constraints and reporting requirements, as described in Chapter 4. Also, as soon as your child becomes a legal adult—18 in most states—he or she will be in charge of the money, and let's be honest, how many 18 year olds do you know who are prepared to manage even a modestly sized financial windfall? Again, making a living trust your policy beneficiary is one strategy for getting around this problem.

Retirement Assets

You probably own at least one type of retirement asset, most likely an employer-sponsored 401(k), to which you contribute pretax dollars; an employer-sponsored Roth 401(k), a relatively new option funded with after-tax dollars; a traditional individual retirement account (IRA), which is funded with pretax dollars; or a Roth IRA, which is funded with after-tax dollars. Perhaps you have a 403(b), which is the equivalent of a 401(k) in the nonprofit sector, or a 457 plan, which is the equivalent of a 401(k) in the government sector. Also, if you are a small business owner, you may be saving for retirement by participating in a SIMPLE plan (a Savings Incentive Match Plan for Employees) or in a SEP (Simplified Employee Pension).

These are special kinds of IRAs that work much like a traditional IRA.

If you have been diligent about contributing to your retirement account, it may be worth thousands, if not hundreds of thousands of dollars when you retire, which means that when you die your account beneficiary may end up with a substantial sum of money. Just how much your beneficiary will receive will depend in part on whether you have to rely on the account to fund your retirement or to pay for extras during your retirement years. For example, you may have other sources of income, like rental income and stock dividends, which you can use to pay your living expenses and to fund your extras. As a result, you may rarely dip into your retirement savings. On the other hand, you may decide after working hard all of your life that you are going to have fun with that money. For example, you might use most of the funds in the account to travel all over the world or to buy the vacation home you'd always dreamed of owning. How much money your beneficiary will receive will depend upon your plans for the money you've saved.

If your retirement account will be worth a lot when you die, and depending on what you plan to do with those funds, it's a good idea to coordinate your beneficiary designations with the rest of your estate plan. For example, you may decide not to leave your account beneficiary any more of your estate, given what the account will be worth when you die. Also, if you are making your spouse or partner the beneficiary of the account and you are leaving him or her all of the rest of your estate, or the lion's share anyway, it's important to consider how all of those assets will impact the amount of estate taxes your spouse or partner will owe when he or she dies. Up-front planning with the help of an estate planning attorney can mitigate that impact. You should also

How much money your beneficiary will receive will depend upon your plans for the money you've saved.

take steps to minimize the possible impact of those assets on the amount of taxes your estate will owe. Finally, if you want to be sure that when you die, there will be a specific amount of money left in your retirement account(s) for your beneficiary(ies), work with a financial planner to figure out how to achieve your goal.

If you are lucky enough to be participating in your employer's pension retirement plan, assuming you've worked for your employer long enough and are vested in the plan when you retire, your pension beneficiary will automatically receive whatever is left in that fund when you die. For more information about pensions and your estate plan, talk to your estate planning attorney and to your employer's plan administrator. Pensions are subject to their own special laws and are relatively rare these days—often reserved mainly for CEOs, CFOs, and other managers at the very top levels of business.

Pay It Out with a Payable-on-Death Account

A payable-on-death account (POD), also known as a Totten trust, is a simple and low-cost way to put the money from your bank account, a savings bond, or a U.S. Treasury security in trust for one or more designated beneficiaries. In some states a brokerage account can also be a POD account.

To set up a POD account, all you need to do is fill out a form that can be obtained at the financial institution where the account will be located. The form will ask you to designate an account beneficiary. You can designate more than one. Once the POD account is established, you'll have complete access to the account assets while you're alive, and you can also cancel the account if you want. When you die, whatever is left in the account automatically transfers to your beneficiary(ies).

However, if you live in a community property state, the funds in your POD account will be treated as community property, assuming you established it during your marriage. Therefore, your surviving spouse will be legally entitled to half of the account funds when you die, unless he or she waives that right so that everything in the account can go to your designated beneficiary(ies). Also, if you established the account before your marriage, but you make deposits to it while you are married, a portion of the account funds will be treated as community property, and your spouse will be entitled to half of them upon your death. Additionally, in some separate property states, your surviving spouse may also be entitled to a share of the value of your POD account. If you are married and you live in a separate property state, talk to an estate planning attorney to find out what your state's laws say about spouses and POD accounts.

If you make a minor child the beneficiary of a POD account, you must designate an adult to act as the account custodian. This person will manage the account assets on behalf of your child after your death. It may make sense to designate the person you've named as your child's property guardian in your will. Once the child becomes a legal adult, the custodian's responsibilities will end. Therefore, you may not want to use a POD account to transfer a lot of property to a child.

If you fail to designate an account custodian, one of three things will happen at your death:

1. The account funds will be transferred to your surviving spouse (or the child's other parent if you are not

When you make an inter vivos gift, your beneficiaries get to benefit from your estate now, rather than having to wait until after you die.

married to one another), to be held until your child becomes a legal adult.

2. The account assets will be turned directly over to your child, assuming that the assets are not worth very much.

3. Your child's other parent (or personal guardian) will have to ask the court to be appointed guardian of the funds in the POD account during the probate process.

Inter Vivos Gift Giving—Give Your Stuff Away Now, Not Later

You don't have to wait until you die to play Santa Claus to the special people in your life. As part of your estate planning, you can give your assets away while you are alive through inter vivos gift giving—and lower the taxable value of your estate at the same time. When you make an inter vivos gift, your beneficiaries get to benefit from your estate now, rather than having to wait until after you die. Plus, you get the pleasure of watching your beneficiaries enjoy and benefit from what you have given to them, assuming of course that you'll be happy with what they do with your inter vivos gifts!

There are federal restrictions on the amount of inter vivos gifts you can give to a single individual (other than your spouse) each calendar year. If you exceed this limit, the excess amount may cause your estate to owe federal estate taxes. Chapter 2 explains how inter vivos gift giving can impact your potential tax liability. If you want to give away a large portion of your estate while you are alive, it's essential that you plan your gifts with the help of an estate planning attorney in order to minimize any potential negative tax impact on your estate and on the estate of your surviving spouse or partner, as well.

Custodial Accounts for Kids-Only Gifting

Custodial accounts are a special vehicle for making inter vivos gifts to minors only. Depending on whether your state has adopted the Uniform Gifts to Minors Act or the Uniform Transfers to Minors Act (most states have adopted the latter), you can transfer cash, securities including stocks and bonds, annuities, life insurance, and even real estate to a custodial account for the benefit of a child. Although you can establish a custodial account through your will, for the account to be a will substitute, you must set it up outside your will.

When you set up a custodial account, you must designate an account custodian to manage the account assets on behalf of your designated beneficiary. This account custodian can be you, the child's parent or property guardian, or some other adult. While the child is a minor, the custodian is entitled to take money out of the account to spend on the child's behalf, reinvest any income the account assets may generate, buy or sell any stocks that may be in the account, collect rents from rental property that may have been transferred to the account, and so on. If you manage a custodial account on behalf of one of your children, however, you cannot use the account funds to pay for things that are your responsibility to pay for as a parent, including your child's food, clothing, and shelter.

When the beneficiary of the account becomes a legal adult, the custodian's job will end, and the child will have full control over whatever is left in the account. In some states, however, you can opt to have the custodial account continue until your beneficiary turns 25. Even so, like POD accounts, custodial accounts are generally not good vehicles for transferring a substantial amount of assets to a young adult. Chapter 9 provides more information about custodial accounts.

An ethical will is a wonderful way to create a personal and lasting legacy.

An Ethical Will—Your Lasting Personal Legacy

You are more than just the money you've earned and the assets that you've purchased with those funds. You are also your life experiences, memories, family traditions, religious values, ethics, hopes, dreams, and all of the other intangibles that make you who you are. Together, these intangibles comprise your personal legacy—a legacy that you can pass on to your loved ones when you die, just like you can pass on your financial legacy.

An ethical will is a wonderful way to create a personal and lasting legacy. Preparing an ethical will is a highly personal act that reflects your personality, your beliefs, your feelings and emotions, and your life. It can also be a personally rewarding process, helping you gain new insights into yourself, reach closure on emotionally painful or traumatic life experiences, tie up any loose ends with those you are leaving behind, and express emotions that you may have trouble verbalizing.

Here are some of the specific things you can do with your ethical will:

- Keep your memory alive.
- Share your wisdom and values with your children and grandchildren.
- Explain the role that religion has played in your life.
- Express the hopes and dreams you have for each of your children.
- Reach out to people from whom you are estranged.
- Apologize and make amends to people you have hurt or harmed in some way.
- Tell the special people in your life exactly what they mean to you.
- Convey your personal history.

■ Reflect on the special memories you have of your marriage or of your life with your partner.

Writing an Ethical Will

You may never have heard of an ethical will. However, they have actually been around since biblical days. Today, interest in ethical wills is increasing, in part because baby boomers are beginning to confront their own mortality, and many of them are looking for a way to pass on to their children and grandchildren something more meaningful and lasting than their money, their homes, their 401(k)s, their household effects, and so on.

If you write an ethical will, you don't have to worry about making sure that it meets certain legal requirements, nor will it go through the probate process after you die. That's because an ethical will is not a legal document; it's a heartfelt, highly personal "letter" that most people use to convey their personal and religious values and life-lessons-learned to their children and grandchildren to help shape their characters.

Because ethical wills don't have to comply with special standards, you can use yours to convey whatever you want. Also, it can be long or short, handwritten or typed, it can include poetry, religious quotes, or anything else you think will help make your points. One practical note, however, it's a good idea to write it using acid-free paper. That way it won't disintegrate and fade over the years, and future generations of your family can read your words and benefit from your thoughts and wisdom.

If you decide to write an ethical will for someone you care about, you may want to share with them your thoughts about:

■ What makes make them special.
■ The love and affection you feel for them.

A multitude of resources are available to help you write an ethical will and create your personal legacy.

- What makes you most proud of them.
- Important events in your life.
- Memories of special moments you've shared.
- Your family's history and heritage.
- Your hopes and dreams for their future.
- Anything else of importance and value that will be lost when you die.

In addition, if you are the head of a family business and a family member will run it after your death, you can use your ethical will to convey the philosophy that shaped your management style, discuss your business values—which may include honesty, openness, collegiality, community service, and so on—and explain why those values are important to you and how you applied them in your business life.

Resources for writing an ethical will. A multitude of resources are available to help you write an ethical will and create your personal legacy. Some of them are described here, but you'll find many more by taking a trip to the bookstore and by searching the Web.

- *Ethical Wills (www.ethicalwill.com).* This website offers guidelines for writing an ethical will and highlights helpful books and free ethical will-writing software. It also offers information about upcoming ethical will-writing workshops and seminars in various parts of the country, as well as other ethical will resources. The site also features examples of ethical wills to help illustrate what you can do with yours.
- *Ethical Wills,* 2nd edition, by Barry K. Baines (Perseus Books). This ethical will classic is an easy-to-understand and invaluable resource.

■ *So That Your Values Live On: Ethical Wills and How to Prepare Them* by Jack Riemer and Nathaniel Stampfer (Jewish Lights Publishing). This inspirational and often touching book features many examples of ethical wills written by a variety of people from different periods. They include letters, poems, and more legal-sounding documents.

■ *Women's Lives, Women's Legacies: Passing Your Beliefs and Blessings to Future Generations: Creating Your Own Spiritual-Ethical Will* by Rachael Freed (Fairview Press). This creative book encourages women to reflect on their lives and to put their thoughts on paper by providing them with a systematic way to examine their pasts, presents, and futures.

This chapter took you beyond wills and living trusts by giving you a rundown on other estate planning tools you can use to convey your assets to your loved ones. These include owning property as joint tenants, giving away your assets while you are alive, and making your loved ones the beneficiaries of your life insurance policies, retirement assets, and payable-on-death accounts. It also discussed setting up custodial accounts for the benefit of your minor children. You should now be aware of how each of these estate planning tools works, along with their pros and cons. You now also know that you can use an ethical will, to convey your personal legacy to your loved ones. That legacy may include, among other things, your values, your personal history, your religious convictions, your memories, and more.

Planning for Your Family

Estate Planning for Spouses and Unmarried Couples

Chapter 8

Your marriage vows may have concluded with the words "until death do us part," but if you are like most married people, you don't believe that your obligation to your spouse should end at your death. Therefore, one of your primary estate planning goals, especially if you're the primary breadwinner in your family, is almost certainly to make sure that your spouse will be provided for financially if you are the first to die. Most unmarried couples who are in committed relationships want to do the same thing. The challenge, however, is deciding how best to do that.

You may do that by building your estate plan on a will and making your spouse or unmarried partner the main beneficiary (maybe the only beneficiary). You may also own such assets as your bank and brokerage accounts, vehicles, boats, and real estate together as *joint tenants with the right of survivorship*, so that if you die first your share of those assets will automatically pass to your spouse or partner outside your will (joint ownership is covered in more detail in Chapter 7). And you may make your spouse or partner the beneficiary of your retirement accounts and your life insurance policies. If this is the way that you plan for your spouse or partner, then he or she will inherit your assets with *no strings attached* and, for better or worse, will be free to do whatever he or she wants with them. This may include spending all of them, investing them, wasting them, losing them to creditors, giving them away as inter vivos gifts, leaving them to beneficiaries in his or her own estate plan, and so on.

For any number of reasons, however, you may be uncomfortable giving your spouse or unmarried partner such total control over the inheritance, and you may feel that doing so is neither a loving nor a responsible way to include him or her in your estate plan. Maybe, for example, your husband, wife, or unmarried partner is a poor or inexperienced money manager, is in declining health, or lacks good judgment. Therefore, you may prefer to provide for him or her using a testamentary trust that you'll set up and fund through your will. In large part, the terms and conditions that will apply to the trust assets and income will depend on the particular kind of testamentary trust you set up. Chapter 4 explains how testamentary trusts work.

If you build your estate plan on a living trust instead of a will, you'll have similar options for providing for your surviving spouse or partner. As explained in Chapter 6, your living trust will probably hold your assets, as well as the ones owned by your spouse or partner. Your trust document may provide that if you die first, all of those assets will remain in the trust for the benefit of your spouse or partner, with no terms or conditions on what he or she can do with them. However, you may prefer to limit your spouse or partner's access to the trust income or assets, or believe that it would be better for him or her not to be responsible for the trust. In this case, you can stipulate in the trust agreement that when you die, your share of the trust property must be transferred to one or more new trusts, and you'll name your spouse or partner the beneficiary of those trust(s). As with a testamentary trust, the terms and conditions of the trust(s) will depend on the particular type of trust(s) you decide to set up.

Later in this chapter, in the "When You May Want to Entrust Your Spouse or Your Unmarried Partner to a Trust" section, specific examples are given of providing for your spouse or partner using a trust, whether it be a testamentary or a living trust. Then, in the "Types of Trusts to Consider" section, the types of trusts that spouses and unmarried partners commonly use to take care of one another are described. Trusts that can take care of your spouse or partner and also save on estate taxes are discussed, as well.

When you make your spouse or partner the beneficiary of your will, he or she will receive whatever assets you've left to him or her as direct distributions if you are the first to die.

Your Will and Your Spouse or Unmarried Partner

When you make your spouse or partner the beneficiary of your will, he or she will receive whatever assets you've left to him or her as direct distributions if you are the first to die. When you prepare your will, you'll spell out the specific assets that you are leaving to your spouse or partner, and/or you'll make him or her the residuary beneficiary of your will. As the residuary beneficiary, your spouse or partner will inherit all of the assets that you don't leave in your will to a specific beneficiary and that aren't transferred outside your will via some other legal means.

You will also designate one or more alternate beneficiaries for each of the specific assets you leave to your spouse or partner, as well as at least one alternate residuary beneficiary, assuming that your spouse is your first choice for residuary beneficiary. If you have children, you may make them the alternate beneficiaries, which means that they will inherit the assets you've left to your spouse or partner if he or she does not survive you.

It's a good idea to include a simultaneous death clause in your will, just in case the two of you die together. Your spouse or partner's will should include this clause too. That way, if the two of you die together, your assets will be distributed as though each of you survived the other. In other words, the assets you earmarked in your will for your spouse or partner won't pass to his or her estate, and the same will be true for the assets in the will of your spouse or partner.

Your Retirement Assets and Your Spouse or Unmarried Partner

Most married couples and committed unmarried couples make one another the beneficiary of their retirement accounts, which may include tax-deferred assets like an IRA, a 401(k), a Keogh, a SEP, or a pension. (They are tax deferred because you don't pay income taxes on the funds that you deposit in these accounts until you withdraw money from the accounts.)

If you make your spouse the beneficiary of your retirement account(s) when you die, whatever is left in the account(s) will automatically transfer to him or her and won't have to go through probate first. Once your spouse receives the funds, he or she can roll them over into an IRA, and your spouse won't have to begin taking money out the account until he or she turns 70½, at which time your spouse will be taxed on the withdrawals. The additional income could push him or her into a higher tax bracket.

If your spouse doesn't roll over the proceeds from your tax-deferred retirement accounts, then he or she will have to begin taking distributions from the account in the year that you die, as well as claiming that income on his or her income tax return. Also, if you leave your retirement assets to your partner (or to someone else who isn't your spouse), he or she must begin taking distributions in the year that you die. Your partner doesn't have the rollover option that spouses do.

Because your spouse or partner will own your retirement assets when you die, he or she will determine what happens to them—how they are used and who will end up with whatever benefits remain when he or she dies. Also, the value of those assets will be included in his or her taxable estate.

To avoid creating tax problems for your spouse or partner and to maintain control over your retirement assets after your death, transfer them to a trust rather than directly distributing them to your spouse or partner. This would mean that the trust would own those assets, not your spouse or partner. Your spouse or partner could receive income from the trust for the rest of his or her life, but you could reserve the right to decide what should happen to the remaining trust assets when he or she dies.

If your retirement assets include a Roth IRA and your spouse or partner is the beneficiary of that account too, he or she will not owe any taxes on withdrawals from the account. That's because a Roth IRA is not a tax-deferred retirement asset. In other words, your Roth was funded with after-tax dollars.

Life insurance plays an important role in the estate plans of most married couples and committed unmarried couples.

Your Life Insurance Policy and Your Spouse or Partner

Life insurance plays an important role in the estate plans of most married couples and committed unmarried couples. You may have purchased a life insurance policy and made your spouse or partner the policy beneficiary, which means that when you die, the policy proceeds will be paid directly to him or her. You may have purchased the policy so that your spouse or partner will have funds to cover the costs of probating your estate or to make certain that your spouse or partner will have plenty of money to live on after your death.

Though making your spouse or partner the beneficiary of your life insurance may seem like the loving thing to do, if the value of the policy's death benefits—the amount of money that will be paid to your spouse or partner—is substantial, you may want to consider making an irrevocable life insurance trust the policy beneficiary instead. That way, you can control through your trust instructions the amount of access your spouse or partner has to the policy proceeds and what he or she can do with those funds. How this kind of trust works is explained in the "Types of Trusts to Consider" section of this chapter.

When You May Want to Entrust Your Spouse or Your Unmarried Partner to a Trust

As discussed at the beginning of this chapter, you may not believe that transferring your assets directly to your surviving spouse or partner when you die is the right thing to do. You may prefer to transfer your assets to a trust for the benefit of your spouse or partner. The following are some reasons why you may want to take care of your spouse with a trust.

You Have Children from a Prior Marriage

If you leave all of your assets directly to your spouse or partner, then your spouse or partner can do whatever he or she wants with them after you die. As a result, your children could end up with nothing.

Your Assets Will Create a Future Estate Tax Problem for Your Spouse

Though the marital tax deduction lets you leave all of your assets to your surviving spouse tax-free, no matter how much those assets are worth, when your spouse dies, your spouse will be unable to take advantage of that same deduction (unless he or she remarries of course). This means that if the assets in his or her estate (whatever is left of what you passed on to your spouse, as well as whatever assets your spouse may own individually) are greater than his or her federal estate tax exemption, then your spouse's estate will owe taxes on the difference. The marital tax deduction does not apply to unmarried couples.

You Want to Ensure That Your Spouse or Unmarried Partner Will Be Eligible for Government Benefits

If your spouse or partner becomes disabled or needs nursing home care, you will want him or her to be eligible for Medicaid, Supplemental Security Income (SSI), and other income-eligible government benefits, which are only available to people of very limited financial means. However, if you make your spouse or partner the beneficiary of a special needs trust, you get to "have your cake and eat it too," because you can transfer to the trust whatever assets you want your spouse or partner to benefit from, and those assets won't make your spouse or partner ineligible for the government benefits he or she may need.

You Don't Want Your Assets to Go through Probate

For a variety of reasons, probate and spouses or unmarried partners are not always a good mix. First, assets that are probated become part of the public record, and companies that are selling financial products like life insurance, annuities, long-term care insurance, and mortgage products often scour those records, prospecting for people who have recently received an inheritance. As a result, they may hound your spouse or partner in an effort to try to convince him or her to buy what they are selling. If your spouse or partner is not financially savvy, he or she may end up purchasing financial products that he or she doesn't need. Also, the friends and relatives of your spouse or partner may review the probate court records to learn what he or she inherited from you, and then begin asking your spouse or partner for handouts or loans that they have no intention of repaying.

Other Reasons to Take Care of Your Spouse or Partner With a Trust

You may also reach the conclusion that arranging a trust for your spouse or partner is a good idea because:

- **Your spouse or partner is an inexperienced money manager.** During your relationship, you've always paid the bills, handled the banking, worked with the broker, done the taxes, and so on.
- **Your spouse or partner is an overspender.** Your spouse or partner goes through money like it's water. You are worried that if you leave your assets to him or her in your will, eventually your spouse or partner may not have enough money to maintain the kind of lifestyle you want him or her to have, much less have anything left to pass on to your children.

- **Your spouse or partner has health problems, such as a chronic physical illness, a serious mental health problem, or an addiction to alcohol or drugs.** These problems may mean that your spouse or partner has trouble managing his or her day-to-day activities and making sound decisions on a timely basis.
- **Your spouse or partner is naïve and gullible.** Your spouse or partner can't tell a good deal from a rip-off. You worry that your spouse or partner may fall for financial scams or put his or her inheritance in overly risky investments.
- **Your spouse or partner is a pushover.** Your spouse or partner can't say no whenever your adult children ask him or her for money, and some of them make a habit of asking.

An estate planning attorney who has trust experience can tell you which trusts might be best for you.

Types of Trusts to Consider

The trusts described in this section represent the kinds of trusts that spouses and unmarried couples most often use to provide for one another, although some of the trusts can only be used by married couples. Each of the trusts described here can be set up through your will or through your living trust. Some of them help save on estate taxes, too. An estate planning attorney who has trust experience can tell you which trusts might be best for you.

Marital Deduction Trust

You can transfer as many assets as you want to this trust for the benefit of your spouse, and because of the marital deduction, your estate will owe no estate taxes on these assets when you die, regardless of what they may be worth. Your spouse will decide who will inherit the assets when he or she dies. However, the trust assets will be included in your spouse's taxable estate, so depending on their value, they could create a future estate tax problem for him or her. Therefore, a marital deduction trust, which is also referred to as an *A trust* or *survivor's trust*, is often coupled with a *B trust*, commonly known as a *bypass trust*, so that each spouse can transfer his or her estate tax-free. How an A/B trust works is explained later in this chapter. Unmarried couples cannot use this kind of trust because they are not entitled to the federal marital deduction.

Qualified Terminable Interest Property (QTIP) Trust

If you want your spouse or partner to benefit from your estate when you die, but you don't want him or her to be able to include your assets in his or her own estate plan, then a QTIP trust may be just the ticket. As the beneficiary of a QTIP trust, your spouse or partner will be entitled to receive income from the trust during his or her lifetime, and depending on the terms of the trust, your spouse or partner may also be able to receive some of the trust assets. You'll control which assets and how much of the assets your spouse or partner can have access to through the trust agreement.

A QTIP trust is popular with parents who have children from a prior marriage because the trust allows them to ensure that when their spouse or partner dies, their assets will go to their children. The main drawback associated with a QTIP trust is that if your surviving spouse or partner is long-lived or if you die while your spouse or partner is still quite young, it may be many years before your children will benefit from the trust assets.

When a couple has a large estate, a QTIP is often combined with an A/B trust to minimize their estate taxes.

Spendthrift Trust

As its name implies, this kind of trust is a great way to take care of a spouse or partner with a spending problem. You can also use it to provide for a spouse or partner who doesn't know the first thing about managing money or whose access to either the trust assets or the income they may generate is a bad idea. When you make your spouse or partner the beneficiary of a spendthrift trust, he or she will have absolutely no access to any of the trust assets or to the trust income (except as you decide). The trustee will dole out money to your spouse or partner, pay their living expenses, and so on, according to your trust instructions. Furthermore, the creditors of your spouse or partner won't be able to get their mitts on any of the trust assets, although they can collect any past-due debts your spouse or partner may owe by going after the income that he or she has already received from the trust.

Special Needs Trust

If your spouse or partner has a serious mental or physical disability or a serious chronic illness, you should think about setting up a special needs trust or supplemental needs trust for him or her. With this kind of trust, your spouse or partner can benefit from your assets without becoming ineligible for important government programs like Medicaid and SSI, which he or she may be currently participating in or may want to participate in sometime in the future. (By the way, Medicaid not only provides basic health care to low-income people, but also helps pay for their nursing home care.) Normally, only people with low incomes and few, if any, assets are eligible for these programs. This means that your spouse or partner would probably be ineligible for them if you

An A/B trust is the most popular kind of estate tax minimization trust.

left him or her even a relatively small amount of your assets directly.

For your spouse or partner to be eligible for these government benefits, you must set up the trust before he or she turns 65. Also, the trust must meet very specific criteria including:

- The trustee must have total control over the trust assets, and your spouse or partner cannot be the trustee.
- The trust can only be used to pay for goods and services not covered by the government programs.
- The trustee cannot distribute any of the trust income or assets directly to your spouse or partner.
- The trust agreement must include certain very specific language. For example, at a minimum, the agreement should clearly state that the trust will provide "supplemental and extra care" to your spouse or partner over and above what the government will provide, and that the trust is not a basic support trust. If your trust agreement is not worded exactly right, the assets in the trust will simply replace whatever government benefits your spouse or partner may receive, not augment them.

A/B Trust

An A/B trust is the most popular kind of estate tax minimization trust. It's commonly used by married couples whose combined assets are equal to or greater than the total amounts of their individual federal estate tax exemptions. The trust allows both spouses or partners to make maximum use of these exemptions in order to pass on to their beneficiaries—their children usually—the maximum amount of assets tax-free. Unmarried couples can also use A/B trusts.

If you are married and you die first and simply leave everything to your surviving spouse through your will or living trust, your estate won't owe any federal estate taxes because of the federal marital deduction. However, you would be creating a future tax problem for your spouse if the value of the assets in your estate exceeded the amount of your spouse's future tax exemption when he or she died. This would also be a problem if the combined value of your assets plus your spouse's own assets were greater than that exemption. If that were the case, your spouse's estate would owe taxes on the difference between the value of his or her taxable estate and the exemption amount. This would mean that your spouse's beneficiaries—possibly your children—would end up with less of his or her estate.

Here is an example that illustrates this problem: Let's assume that you die in 2009 with an estate that is worth $2 million, and let's assume that your spouse has $150,000 of individual assets. If you leave your entire estate to your spouse when you die, your estate won't owe any federal estate taxes because of the marital deduction. So far so good. However, let's also assume that your spouse dies in 2011 and leaves that same $2 million dollars in assets plus his or her $150,000 worth of assets to your children. In other words, your children inherit $2,150,000. Assuming that Congress has not changed the tax code, this would mean that a whopping $632,500 in estate taxes would be owed on your spouse's estate:

$2.15 million (value of estate)
− $1 million (the federal unlimited tax
  exemption in 2011 under current law)
= $1.15 million

$1.15 million
× 55% (the tax rate in 2011 under current law)
= $632,500

Note: These calculations will change if Congress does what many expect it will do in 2009 and increases the amount of the tax exemption for 2011 and future years. If that happens and you've already set up an A/B trust based on current estate tax law, you need to work with your estate planning attorney to review the trust in accordance with the new law.

With an A/B trust, however, when the first spouse dies (let's assume it's you), assets equal in value to the amount of your federal estate tax exemption will be transferred from your estate (through your living trust or through your will) to an irrevocable B trust. While your surviving spouse is alive, he or she will be entitled to all of the income generated by the trust assets.

In addition, depending on how you word the trust agreement, your spouse may be able to use the trust assets to pay for his or her basic needs and for the needs of any minor children you may have together. Basic needs are generally defined as "health, education, support, and maintenance" and/or $5,000 from the trust or five percent of its value—whichever is greater—every year for any reason. However, your spouse will be unable to give away any of the assets, borrow against them, sell them, or decide what will happen to them when he or she dies—you decide that. Therefore, at the death of your spouse, all of the assets in the B trust will transfer to your designated beneficiaries or will be transferred into another trust for their benefit.

Meanwhile, at the same time that your B trust is funded, any assets over the amount of your tax exemption will be transferred to a revocable A trust. This trust will be for the benefit of your surviving spouse. These assets will transfer to the trust tax-free because of the marital tax deduction. If your spouse has any individual assets, they will be in the trust, too. Your spouse will have complete control over the trust, including the right to decide what will happen to the trust assets when he or she dies. When that happens, your spouse's estate will owe no estate taxes either, assuming that the value of those assets does not exceed the amount of his or her exemption.

Although an A/B trust can be an attractive option for couples of any age with large estates, it tends to be a better choice for older couples—spouses who are 50 years of age or older—than it is for younger couples or when one of the spouses is significantly younger than the other. This is because younger couples don't usually want to tie up a significant amount of their assets in an irrevocable bypass trust. Remember, those assets won't be available to the beneficiaries of that trust until the second spouse dies. Therefore, if you and your spouse have a large estate but you are relatively young, or if you are married to a much younger spouse, talk with your estate planning attorney about other tax minimization strategies you might want to consider for now.

Life Insurance Trust

Rather than making your spouse or partner the beneficiary of your life insurance policy, you can transfer the policy to an irrevocable life insurance trust and designate him or her as the beneficiary of the trust. That way, you can control what can be done with the policy proceeds, as well as what will happen to any funds that remain in the trust when you die. In addition, because the trust, not you, will own the policy, the policy's value won't be included in your taxable estate, assuming that the policy is transferred to the trust at least three years prior to your death. It won't be included in your spouse or partner's estate either.

If you set up and fund the trust while you are alive, you can pay the policy premiums by making a gift of money to the trust each year. Also, you can transfer additional money to the trust in order to purchase more life insurance, if you want. A word of warning, however: Don't make yourself the trustee of the trust. If you do, the policy value will be counted as part of your taxable estate when you die.

Prenuptial and Postnuptial Agreements and Your Estate Plan

If you and your spouse negotiated a prenuptial agreement before your marriage or a postnuptial agreement after your marriage, the agreement may have preestablished what each of you will and won't inherit from the other. Or you may have waived your rights to inherit at least a minimum amount of one another's estates. You also may have used the agreement to alter your individual marital property rights.

For example, one or both of you may have agreed to turn some of your separate property into joint property with the right of survivorship so that when the first spouse dies, the other spouse will automatically own all of that property. Also, if you live in a community property state, one or both of you may have agreed to turn all or part of your separate property into community property, or vice versa. Assuming it's a legally binding document, your estate plan must reflect the terms of your prenuptial or postnuptial agreement, unless the two of you later agreed to cancel the agreement after you signed it.

If you and your spouse decide to predetermine your inheritance rights using a prenuptial or postnuptial agreement, always consult with an estate planning attorney so that you make the right decisions. Otherwise, you may end up creating a lot of problems for whichever spouse survives the other.

Disinheriting Your Spouse

Though it rarely happens, you may not want to leave any of your assets to your spouse or may not want to make him or her the primary beneficiary of your estate plan. Among other reasons, you may reach this decision because you are estranged from one another and only staying together for the sake of your young kids or because you don't think that your spouse needs any of your assets to be financially secure after your death. That might be the case, for example, if your spouse earns a substantial salary and has a bundle in his or her retirement accounts, or if your spouse is your family's primary breadwinner, or if your spouse received a large inheritance or a very substantial divorce settlement when his or her previous marriage ended.

Disinheriting a spouse tends to be easier said than done. If you live in a separate property state, for example, your surviving spouse is legally entitled to a minimum amount of your assets when you die, also referred to as an *elective share* or a *forced share*. Though the process varies from state to state, your spouse will have to fill out a special form to receive his or her elective share and file it with your area's probate court. He or she will have a limited amount of time to do so—generally it's no more than six months.

The amount of the elective share also varies by state. However, it will be some percentage of the value of some portion of your estate—either a percentage of your probate estate or of your probate and *augmented estate*. Depending on your state, your augmented estate may include the value of some of your nonprobate assets,

Disinheriting a spouse tends to be easier said than done.

like your life insurance policy, retirement benefits, property that you own jointly with someone else, assets that are in a living trust, and maybe even the value of assets that you gave away as inter vivos gifts in the years immediately prior to your death.

If you want to disinherit your spouse or if you intend to pass on to him or her just a very small amount of your estate, your estate planning attorney will probably recommend that you leave your spouse assets equal to the amount of your state's elective share instead. If your surviving spouse were to take his or her elective share, that amount would come out of the inheritance that you are leaving to one or more of your other estate planning beneficiaries. This could mean that some of your estate planning goals might not be achieved. By leaving your spouse the minimum amount that he or she is legally entitled to, you control exactly which assets he or she ends up with and, in the process, you preserve the integrity of your estate plan.

If you live in a community property state, you can't disinherit your surviving spouse because he or she legally owns a one-half interest in all of the money either of you earned during your marriage, as well as all of the assets you acquired during that time. However, you could choose to leave your half interest in your community property to someone other than your spouse, which would mean that your surviving spouse would not own 100 percent of those assets when you die. Arizona, California, Idaho, Louisiana, Nevada, New Mexico, Texas, Washington, and Wisconsin are all community property states.

Estate Planning for Your Same-Sex Partner

In most states, same-sex partners don't have the same legal rights that married couples have when it comes to their estate plans. For example, if you are in a same-sex relationship and you die *intestate* (without a will), assuming that you didn't transfer all of your assets to a living trust and make your partner the trust beneficiary before your death, your partner won't be legally entitled to any of what you own. Instead, all of your assets will go to your children, or if you don't have any, to your parents, your siblings, and so on. Also, you don't have the right to transfer to your partner an unlimited amount of your assets estate tax–free, and your partner doesn't have a right to visit you in the hospital when you are critically ill or injured. However, with the appropriate planning, you can approximate the estate planning rights and benefits that married couples get automatically.

Here is another important reason to have an estate plan when you are in a same-sex relationship: If you become incapacitated and can't make your own decisions about your finances and your medical care, unless you prepare the appropriate legal documents, a probate judge will appoint someone to make those decisions for you, and the judge probably won't pick your partner.

STATES OFFERING BENEFITS TO SAME-SEX COUPLES

Some states offer marriagelike benefits to same-sex couples. At the time this book was written they are:

■ **Massachusetts.** This state permits same-sex partners to marry and to enjoy all of the same state-level inheritance and hospital visitation rights that heterosexual married couples have.

■ **Connecticut, New Hamshire, New Jersey, Oregon, and Vermont.** These states allow same-sex couples to enter into civil unions. Couples who are in civil unions are legally entitled to some of the same state-level rights that married couples enjoy when it comes to inheritance and hospital visitation. However, the specific rights vary from state to state.

■ **California, Maine, Washington State, and the District of Columbia.** Same-sex couples residing in these three states and in the District of Columbia can enter into domestic partnerships. Generally, those who do are legally entitled to all of the same state-level rights as married couples, with a few variations. For example, in California, which is a community property state, domestic partners have all of the community property rights that married couples have.

■ **Hawaii.** This state has a reciprocal beneficiaries law. It gives same-sex couples who register as reciprocal beneficiaries some of the same rights as married couples.

A civil union and a domestic partnership are generally the same thing, though in some states, the term *domestic partnership* applies to heterosexual unmarried couples as well as same-sex couples. The specific rights that come with these two types of formal relationships vary from state to state.

State laws regarding same-sex relationships are in flux. Therefore, even though your state may not be included on the preceding list, its legislature may have passed a law since this book was written giving you and your partner some inheritance and hospital visitation rights. It's also possible that, if your state is on the list, your state's legislature took action after this book was written to restrict your rights. For up-to-date information about exactly what rights you and your partner do and don't have in your particular state, contact an estate planning attorney or the office of your state attorney general. You can also visit the website of the Human Rights Campaign at *www.hrc.org*, where you'll find state-by-state summaries of all existing laws and all pending laws related to same-sex partnership.

This chapter filled you in on the many ways that you can include your spouse or unmarried partner in your estate plan, and it discussed the kinds of issues you may want to consider when you are deciding how best to plan for him or her. You should now have a greater understanding of prenuptial and postnuptial agreements, issues related to disinheriting a spouse, as well as the special estate planning challenges faced by same-sex partners.

Estate Planning for Your Children

Chapter 9

I f you have minor children—children who are younger than 18 or 21, depending on your state—and you die before they are adults, there will be many things that you won't have the opportunity to do with them as they move into adulthood. Though you can do little now to make up for all of the things that your children will miss if you die while they are still young, you *can* help ensure the quality of two aspects of their lives through your estate plan. First, you can ensure that their financial needs will be met. Second, you can ensure that your children will be raised by another caring adult who shares your personal and religious values, as well as your attitudes toward child rearing, if they lose both you and their other parent while they are minors. This other adult will act as their personal guardian. As explained in the personal guardian section of Chapter 4, you must formally name this person in your will.

Your goals will be different if your children are already adults when you prepare your estate plan. Although there are exceptions when it comes to adult children, rather than using your estate plan to make sure that they will be financially secure after you die, you will probably treat your estate plan as a means

You can use your estate plan in many ways to provide for your young children after you die, although some ways are better than others.

of providing your adult children (and their families) with a financial "leg up on life." Because of your estate plan, they may be able to buy a home sooner than they would otherwise, pay cash for their children's college educations, build a substantial retirement nest egg, and generally have a more financially secure life than they would have.

Estate Planning When Your Children Are Minors

You can use your estate plan in many ways to provide for your young children after you die, although some ways are better than others. For example, you can:

- **Use your will to transfer your assets to your surviving spouse or partner.** You'll probably make your children the secondary beneficiaries of your will, and your spouse or partner will probably make them the primary beneficiaries of his or her own estate plan.
- **Make your children primary beneficiaries of your will.** You can leave assets directly to your children in your will. If you die while they are still minors, the person you designated in your will to act as their property guardian will manage their assets. Chapter 4 discusses property guardians in more detail.
- **Establish a custodial account for each of your children.** You can set up and fund this kind of account while you are alive or after your death through your will or your living trust.
- **Make your kids the beneficiaries of your life insurance policy.** Your children's property guardian will manage the policy proceeds after your death.
- **Make your minor children the beneficiaries of a testamentary trust.** A testamentary trust is created

through your will. You can use one trust to benefit all of your kids or you can set up separate trusts for each of them.

■ **Take care of your kids through your living trust.** While you are alive, you and your spouse or partner will probably transfer all of your assets to the trust and manage the trust together to benefit yourselves and your kids. If you die or become incapacitated, your surviving spouse or partner will continue managing the trust.

■ **Use your living trust to set up a shared trust or separate trusts for your minor children after your death.** Rather than having all of your assets remain in your living trust if you die when your children are still minors, you can direct that a portion of those assets be transferred to a joint trust for all of your children or to separate trusts.

Take Care of Your Kids through Your Will

You may use your will in two ways to take care of your kids after your death. One way is to leave everything to your spouse or partner, so he or she can use your assets to take care of your children. The other way is to leave your assets directly to your children in your will.

Leave Everything to Your Spouse or Partner

Like a lot of parents, you may be inclined to provide for your children by leaving all of your assets to your surviving spouse or partner in your will. If you do, he or she will have full control over those assets when you die and will be free to spend and invest them however he or she wants. Your spouse or partner will also be free to give those assets to whomever he or she wants in his or her own estate plan.

Although providing for your children this way is simple and easy, and on the surface at least, may seem to make total sense, when you leave everything to your spouse or partner, you are making some assumptions that may or may not be true. The following are just a few possible assumptions.

- **Your spouse or partner will do a good job of managing your assets after you die.** You are also assuming that when it comes to your young children, the financial priorities of your spouse or partner will mirror yours.

- **Your spouse or partner will use his or her own estate plan to make sure that your children will eventually end up with whatever is left of your assets.** In other words, you assume that your surviving spouse or partner won't remarry or enter into an unmarried relationship and leave those assets to his or her new spouse or partner, or decide to own them jointly with the new spouse or partner.

- **Your spouse's new spouse or partner won't have a domineering personality.** If he or she does, your spouse or partner may have little say about how your assets are used, and as a result, your children may not end up with the kind of lifestyle that they would have if you were still alive.

- **Your spouse's next marriage won't end in divorce.** Your spouse could lose much of his or her inheritance in the divorce settlement.

- **Your spouse or partner won't develop financial problems after your death.** If that happens, his or her creditors may collect what your spouse or partner owes to them by taking some of the assets you left to him or her. It's also possible that your spouse or partner could lose them in bankruptcy.

Make Your Kids Beneficiaries of Your Will

If the long list of assumptions in the previous section makes you wince and squirm, then you may prefer to use your will to transfer some of your estate directly to your minor children when you die. However, this option has drawbacks, too. They include the following.

- The assets will have to go through probate before they can begin to benefit your children.
- Your children's property guardian will be subject to state-imposed rules and restrictions regarding what he or she can do with the assets—what they can be spent on and invested in—and his or her activities will be monitored by the probate court. In addition, the property guardian will have to provide the court with regular reports about the status of your children's finances. As a result, information about your children's assets and income will be part of the public record, and the probate court may be a presence in your children's lives for many years, depending on their ages when you die.
- Your children will receive whatever is left of their inheritance once they become legal adults, regardless of what it's worth and whether your children are prepared to manage it.

For all of these reasons, if your children's inheritance is going to be substantial—and especially if it will include complex assets that aren't easy to manage, such

as investment real estate, stocks, and business interests—
you may not want to plan for your minor children by
making them the beneficiaries of your will.

Make Your Children the Beneficiaries of Your Life Insurance Policy

Purchasing life insurance and making your young children
your policy beneficiaries is a very affordable way to leave
them with a large sum of money (the policy death benefit)
when you die. However, it has all of the same disadvantages
associated with making your children the beneficiaries of
your will—the death benefit will be managed by their property guardian, information about the death benefit will be
in the public record, and your children will control whatever is left of that money once they become legal adults.

However, you can steer clear of all of these disadvantages by making an irrevocable life insurance trust,
not your young children, the policy beneficiary. That
way, the policy proceeds will be managed by whomever
you've named as the trustee of the trust, and you'll control when your children can receive whatever is left in the
trust. Furthermore, if federal estate taxes are a concern
for you, by transferring your policy to an irrevocable life
insurance trust, you'll get it out of your taxable estate.

Create Custodial Accounts for Your Kids

Setting up a custodial account for each of your children
(a custodial account can have only one beneficiary) at
your bank or brokerage house and transferring some of
your assets to each of the accounts is another easy and
inexpensive way to include them in your estate plan.

You can fund the accounts while you are alive or after your death through your will or living trust. If you transfer assets to the accounts while you are alive, the assets will be treated as inter vivos gifts, which means that their value won't be included in your taxable estate when you die. Other adults can transfer assets to your children's custodial accounts, too.

The specific kinds of assets you can put in a custodial account depend on whether your state has passed the Uniform Gifts to Minors Act (UGMA) or the Uniform Transfers to Minors Act (UTMA). Under both laws, you can transfer assets such as bank accounts, stocks, mutual funds, insurance policies, and annuities, but if your state adopted the UTMA, you can put real estate in the account, too. To find out which law your state adopted, contact your bank, brokerage firm, or an estate planning attorney. Most states have adopted the UTMA.

When you set up a custodial account, you must designate a *custodian* for the account, who will manage the account assets on your child's behalf (be sure to designate at least one alternate custodian, too). You can be the custodian while you are alive. However, if you die while the account is open, the account assets will be included in your taxable estate.

Some big advantages are associated with custodial accounts, including the following.

■ Your children's custodians won't have to comply with the restrictive rules and onerous reporting requirements that apply to property guardians, which means that the probate court won't be involved in your children's lives. In fact, the account custodians will have nearly complete discretion to manage and invest the assets in the accounts and to use the assets as

Despite their advantages, custodial accounts have drawbacks, too.

they believe are necessary to provide for your young children's basic needs, including their food, shelter, clothing, and medical care. The account custodians can also use these resources to help pay for your children's education.

■ Information about the custodial accounts won't be part of the public record.

Despite their advantages, custodial accounts have drawbacks, too. For example:

■ **Custodial accounts are irrevocable.** Once you transfer assets to a custodial account, you can't take them back. They belong to your child.

■ **Once your child becomes a legal adult, the account will end.** At that point, your young adult children will receive whatever assets are left in their accounts. Therefore, custodial accounts are probably not a good choice if the value of those assets will be substantial and will include stocks, real estate, and other investments that most 18 or 21 year olds are unprepared to manage wisely. However, in a few states, you can keep your children's custodial account open until they turn 25.

■ **You can't designate alternate beneficiaries for a custodial account.** Therefore, if one of your minor children dies before he or she reaches the age at which the account is due to end, the account assets will be in your child's estate and will be distributed according to your state's inheritance law. You'll have no control over what happens to them.

■ **Any income earned by the assets in a custodial account could have income tax consequences for you.** The current federal tax law says that if your child is younger than 19, or a full-time student who is under age 24, and receiving more than half of their income from you, then the first $900 of any unearned income, including income generated by the custodial account assets, won't be taxed. The next $900 will be taxed at your child's ordinary tax rate, which will probably be lower than your rate. (This tax is commonly referred to as the *kiddie tax.*) However, any unearned income over $1,800 will be taxed at *your* ordinary rate, and you will have to file a separate income tax for your child. (These amounts are periodically adjusted for inflation, so check with your CPA or estate planning attorney for the most up-to-date information.) In essence, this means that the income will be added to your taxable income. Consequently, you could end up in a higher tax bracket.

■ **The account assets could affect your child's eligibility for college financial aid.** Under current law, your child's own assets count more than yours do when the amount of financial aid he or she is eligible for is being calculated. Your children could have this same problem if you leave them assets directly in your will or if you make them the beneficiaries of your life insurance policy.

Entrust Your Children to a Trust

If you want to avoid most of the problems associated with the previous options, then a trust is the answer— either a testamentary trust or a living trust. You can control when your children will inherit the trust assets once they've become legal adults, as well as what the trust assets and income can be used for and invested in. This is not just while your children are minors but once they are adults too, assuming that the trusts won't end at that point. The following are some of the many ways that you can use a trust to take care of your children.

Take Care of Your Kids with a Testamentary Trust

If you build your estate plan on a will, you can use a testamentary trust to do exactly what you can with a living trust, with one exception. Because a testamentary trust will only come into existence after you die, it won't take care of your children's financial needs if you or your spouse or partner becomes incapacitated while they are still minors. Also, after your death, any assets that you want in trust must go through probate first, so there will be a delay—maybe as long as a year or more—before the trust can be funded. The delay may not be a problem, however, if your minor children are also the beneficiaries of other assets that won't go through probate, like a custodial account or life insurance. Those assets can be used to provide for them until the probate process is over.

Provide for Your Minor Children through Your Living Trust

If you build your estate plan on a living trust, you and your spouse or partner will transfer your assets to the trust while you are alive. You'll manage the assets for the benefit of everyone in your family, including your minor children, just as you did before the trust existed. When the first spouse dies (let's assume it's you), your surviving spouse or partner will probably continue to manage the trust assets. However, your trust agreement could direct that someone else manage the trust instead, maybe because your spouse or partner isn't a good money manager or is in poor health.

Although it depends on the terms of your trust agreement, if your surviving spouse or partner also dies while your children are minors, it's likely that the remaining trust assets will either be transferred to a single trust that will benefit all of your children, or they'll be divided up among individual trusts—one for each of your young children. The trust assets will be managed by the trustee(s) designated in the trust agreement according to the instructions in that agreement. The trusts will be set up and funded automatically without any court involvement, assuming that all of your instructions are clear and that no one tries to contest the terms of the trust(s). Shared and individual trusts for minor children are discussed later in this chapter.

Use an A/B Trust

If minimizing estate taxes *and* providing for your minor children are your estate planning goals, you can achieve both of them by instructing that when you die, your assets be divided between two trusts—an irrevocable B trust and a revocable A trust. Your minor children will benefit from the B trust assets and income, which will be managed according to your instructions (you can direct that your surviving spouse or partner be entitled to benefit from the trust, too). Your surviving spouse or partner will be the sole beneficiary of the A trust. He or she will control the assets in this trust and any income they may generate and will decide what will happen to them when he or she dies. Chapters 6 and 8 provide additional information about bypass and marital trusts. As both chapters explain, an A/B trust can be set up through your living trust or through your will.

Shared versus Separate Trusts for Minor Children

When you are planning for more than one minor child, you have two broad options: You can fund one trust that they will all benefit from should you and your spouse or partner both die while they are minors, or you can set up a separate trust for each of your children and divide up your assets among the trusts. Each option has its advantages and drawbacks, so you should carefully consider which one is best for your children with the help of an estate planning attorney. There is no one right answer when it comes to young children. To prepare you for that discussion, the following sections summarize the pros and cons of each option.

Using a shared trust. Most parents provide for the establishment of a single trust that will benefit all of their minor children. Usually they give the trustee of the trust broad discretion to use the trust assets and income to pay for their children's shelter, food, clothing, health, education, and their other needs as they arise. In other words, they let the trustee decide exactly how the trust resources will be used and when to spend more on one child than another. This arrangement approximates how you take care of your kids now.

In your trust instructions, you'll indicate when the trust should end and what should happen to the remaining trust assets at that time. However, the issue of when to end the trust can be a bit complicated, especially if the difference between the ages of your oldest and youngest child is large. For example, let's assume that you decide that the trust will end when all of your children have graduated from college or once your youngest child turns 25—whichever occurs first—and that each of your children will receive an equal share of the remaining trust assets at that point. The problem with this arrangement is that your oldest child will receive his or her inheritance much later in life than your youngest child will.

One way to handle this problem, assuming the trust is large enough, is to allow your oldest child (or children) to receive advances on his or her inheritance once that child reaches a certain age or passes a specific milestone. However, to preserve the financial integrity of the trust, it's best to limit the size of each advance, as well as the number of advances that child can take. You can also restrict what your child may use the advances for. If you decide to allow advances, make sure that your trust instructions are very clear that when the trust ends, the total value of the advances your oldest child received will be deducted from the total amount he or she will be entitled to under the terms of the trust.

Depending on the terms of the trust agreement, the trust will end once all of your children have reached a certain age, at which point any remaining trust assets will be distributed to them immediately or over time. The trust could continue to exist to benefit your children long after they have become adults, or the assets could be transferred to separate trusts for each of your adult children.

Using separate trusts. An advantage of using separate trusts to provide for your minor children is that you can customize the terms and conditions of each trust to respond to their individual needs. However, if your children are very young when you prepare your estate plan, what those different needs are may not yet be apparent. Therefore, you may want to initially fund each trust for the same amount and end each trust at the same time, and then modify the terms and conditions of the trusts as your children grow older and their financial needs and differences become more apparent. This can be a risky approach, however, because you may die before you make the appropriate adjustments to the trusts.

Another problem with separate trusts is that you cannot know ahead of time exactly what your children's financial needs will be after your death, and if you

> An advantage of using separate trusts to provide for your minor children is that you can customize the terms and conditions of each trust to respond to their individual needs.

predict wrong, you could end up creating a financial hardship for some of your children. This is because the trustee(s) of your children's separate trusts cannot move assets and income from one trust into another trust in order to respond to your children's changing needs.

As a case in point, consider what happened to Suzy and Marcia, two children whose parents died in a tragic car crash. After their parents died, a separate trust for each girl was set up and funded for the exact same amount. Initially, this arrangement worked just fine. However, during Suzy's senior year of high school, she became very ill, had to have several surgeries, and was in the hospital for long stretches of time. As a result, the cost of her medical care used up most of the funds in her trust, and once she was healthy again, there was very little left to pay for her college education. So Suzy had to enroll in a state college near her home, graduated with almost $50,000 of debt, and had to get a job right away so she could afford to repay what she owed. Marcia, on the other hand, had plenty of money in her trust when it came time for college. She attended an expensive private university, graduated debt-free, and spent the first several months after she graduated traveling around Europe. When she returned home, she used her trust fund to finance her graduate school education. Suzy and Marcia's parents would never have imagined that their decision to set up separate and equal trusts for their two daughters would mean each girl would end up living such different lifestyles.

Estate Planning for Your Adult Children

In many ways, estate planning for adult children is easier than planning for minors because you have more information to work with. Therefore, it's easier to create a plan that reflects the individual realities of each of your children's lives—whether they are level-headed and good money managers, have emotional problems and/or addictions, are all on lucrative career paths, and so on. In contrast, when your children are minors, deciding how your estate plan should treat them once they've become adults is always somewhat of a guessing game.

A Quick Rundown on Ways to Include Your Adult Children in Your Estate Plan

When you are planning for your adult children, you may want to include them in your estate plan. The following are some of the ways to go about doing so.

Make them beneficiaries of your will. This option makes sense if you are completely comfortable letting your children have total control over their inheritances when you die, even if that means that they could be as young as 18 or 21 when that happens. Depending on your estate planning goals and the size of your estate, you may make your children primary beneficiaries of your will together with your spouse, so that all of them will inherit from you when you die. Or you may make your children your spouse's alternate beneficiaries, which means that they will inherit whatever assets you leave to your spouse if he or she is already deceased when you die or if your spouse fails to survive you by whatever number of days you indicate in your will. The number of days is referred to as the survivorship period.

Give your assets to your children while you are alive. This is a good option if you not only want to remove assets from your taxable estate, but you want your children to benefit from some of your wealth before you die. For example, you may decide to give them money for a down payment on a home when they turn 25 or to give each of them a share of your investment portfolio when they turn 30.

Make your adult children the beneficiaries of a testamentary or living trust—one trust for all or separate trusts. This option gives you the opportunity to control what they can do with the trust assets and when they can receive their inheritance. Again, your children and spouse can be the beneficiaries of the same trust with the trust providing for your spouse first and then, upon his or her death, for your adult children. Or you can set up one or more separate trusts just for your children.

Make them the beneficiaries of your life insurance policy, retirement accounts, and any other beneficiary assets you may own. Depending on the terms of your plan, they may receive these assets directly, or you may put the assets in one or more trusts for their benefit.

You may decide to use one estate planning method or a combination of methods for some of your children, and another method or combination of methods for others. Cases in point, two of your children are happy, well-balanced people with successful careers. You feel comfortable leaving them their share of your estate in your will. However, your third child is addicted to drugs and you worry that if you do the same for that child, he or she will spend every penny of the inheritance on drugs and could become a financial burden for your other children. Therefore, you put that child's share of your estate in a spendthrift trust, give him or her no access to the trust income or assets, and direct the trustee of the trust to pay your child's monthly bills and to give him or her a small monthly allowance. This kind of trust and other specialized trusts are discussed later in this chapter as well as in Chapters 6 and 8.

Should Your Adult Children Benefit Equally from Your Estate Plan?

Most parents want their estate plan to be fair to their children, so their first inclination is that each of them should benefit equally from their estate. In reality, however, equal shares may not be a good idea or truly fair. For example, consider each of the following scenarios.

- Your oldest child has made a fortune in the high-tech industry and lives a very comfortable lifestyle. Your youngest child, however, has experienced a lot of unfortunate setbacks in life and is struggling to make ends meet as a single parent.
- One of your children has a debilitating illness that will eventually make it impossible for him to work full-time. The rest of your children are healthy.
- Each of your three children live within 30 minutes of your home. But after your health failed two years ago, only one of them has made time to take you to doctor's appointments, run errands for you, help with minor home repairs, and so on.

If you decide that some of your adult children should receive a smaller share of your estate than others, it's a good idea to explain your decision to them while you are alive because they are probably under the assumption that your plan treats all of them the same. If you're not up-front about your decision, the children who received less of your estate are apt to feel hurt, angry, and confused, and they may take their feelings out on your other children. They may even try to contest

If you decide to put your adult children's inheritance in a trust, you'll have to decide when (or if) they will receive the trust assets.

the terms of your plan. Meanwhile, your other children, out of guilt or even embarrassment, may decide to give some of their inheritance to the siblings who received less of your estate, undermining the rationale behind your decision to treat your children differently. Though sharing the details of your estate plan with your children can't provide you with a 100 percent guarantee that there won't be problems after your death, it can help minimize the potential for trouble.

Deciding When Your Adult Children Should Receive the Assets in Their Trust

If you decide to put your adult children's inheritance in a trust, you'll have to decide when (or if) they will receive the trust assets. The following are some of your options.

Let your children receive all their inheritance in a lump sum as soon as you die. This option comes with the same caveat as leaving everything to your adult children in your will. If they are mature, responsible adults, letting them receive their inheritance right away, no strings attached, can be a good choice. However, if they are immature spendthrifts, have no money management abilities, and so on, it could be a disastrous decision. You should take into account the value and the nature of the assets in their trust(s) when you are deciding whether this option is a good choice for your children. It may not be if the assets are worth a lot and require a special expertise to manage.

Distribute it over time. Rather than letting your children receive their inheritance all at once, you can opt to give it to them over time in installments. For example, you may decide to let your children have one-third of the assets in their trust when you die, another share five years later, and so on. Another option is to tie the amounts they receive to their age. For example, when your children turn 24, they receive one-third of their inheritance, another third at age 28, and the balance at age 30. Staging distributions like this gives your children an opportunity to grow accustomed over time to managing their inheritances and ensures that if they make mistakes early on, they won't be putting their entire inheritance at risk.

Don't give your children any control over their inheritance. Another option is to not distribute any of the trust assets to your adult children. Instead, have the trust(s) pay each of your children a set amount of money every month and/or pay for their basic needs for the rest of their lives or until they reach a certain age. This is a good option if you want to preserve the value of the trust for a future use—to benefit your grandchildren or a charity, for example. You may decide that this is an appropriate option for some of your children, but that you want your other children to be able to control their inheritance sooner or later. This might be a good approach if you are afraid that some of your adult children won't manage their inheritance responsibly, that some of your children have a lot of debt and you don't want their creditors to end up with any of the assets in their trust, or if you are worried about what one of your sons- or daughters-in-law might do with your child's inheritance.

Special Trusts for Your Minor and Adult Children

Some parents face special challenges when they are planning for their minor or adult children. Some of them have already been mentioned in this chapter, as well as in Chapters 6 and 8. This section tells you about

Some parents face special challenges when they are planning for their minor or adult children.

special kinds of trusts that you can set up through your will or living trust to address those challenges.

Planning for a Special Needs Child

If you have a child with a special need—a serious physical or mental disability—he or she may be receiving government benefits such as Supplemental Security Income (SSI) or Medicaid, or may want to receive them in the future. However, participation in such programs requires that your child's income be very low and that your child own very few assets. Therefore, if you give that child any control over his or her inheritance, he or she will probably become ineligible for government assistance. The best way to get around this problem is to set up an irrevocable *special needs trust* (also called a *supplemental needs trust*) to hold that child's share of your estate. Your child will have no control over the trust assets or income. Therefore, assuming that the trust meets all of the federal requirements for a special needs trust, it will have no effect on his or her continued or future eligibility for government benefits. Those requirements are spelled out in Chapter 8.

Protecting Your Child from Himself or Herself

Some of your children may have personal problems that argue against giving them any control over their inheritance. For example, your child may be a horrid money manager, struggle with addictions, have emotional problems that sometimes make it difficult for him or her to function and make wise decisions, be married to a greedy spouse, and so on. So what's the solution? Put the assets you want your problem child to benefit from in a spendthrift trust, and direct the trustee to pay that child's monthly bills out of the trust and/or to give that child a monthly stipend. Plus, here's a nice bonus: Any creditors that your child may owe money to can't go after the assets in the spendthrift trust, although they can collect on their debts by going after any income or assets your child may have received from the trust.

Giving Your Child an Incentive

If you are concerned that receiving an inheritance from you will encourage one of your children to continue certain behaviors that you disapprove of, then you may want to consider an *incentive trust*. An incentive trust will provide your child with a monetary incentive for behaving in accordance with certain standards that are set out in the trust. For example:

- You worry that your slacker son will never become a fully productive member of society, especially as he expects to receive a substantial inheritance. Therefore, you put that inheritance in an incentive trust, and instruct the trustee that for every dollar your son earns each month, the trust should pay him an equal amount. Therefore, the more your son works, the more income he has.

- You want to encourage your drug-addicted child to stay straight. Therefore, you put his or her share of your estate in an incentive trust. You can instruct the trustee to pay your child a set amount of money each month, contingent on your child's providing the trustee with written proof that he or she attended weekly Narcotics Anonymous meetings in the previous month. No attendance, no money. Also, you can authorize the trustee to order your child to submit to random drug testing. If the tests show that your child has been using drugs, your child receives no money from the trust until he or she no longer tests positive for drugs.

You can also use incentive trusts to encourage your children to embrace certain values that you hold dear. Those values might include education, voluntarism, entrepreneurship, and so on. For example, you might provide your children with cash "bonuses" when they graduate from college, get a master's degree, spend a certain number of hours each year volunteering, begin their own business, and so on.

There is a caveat associated with incentive trusts! To truly motivate the beneficiaries of this kind of trust, the trust's terms and conditions must be clear, fair, and realistic, and should not sound heavy-handed or coercive, as though you are trying to micromanage your child. Otherwise, the trust may not have the effect that you hoped for. Therefore, if you want to include an incentive trust in your estate plan, hire an estate planning attorney who has specific experience setting up this kind of trust.

Disinheriting a Child

The decision to disinherit a child by not including him or her in your will or trust is almost never an easy one, but you may decide that it's the right one for you. For example, you may make the decision to disinherit because you disapprove of your child's lifestyle or values, you've had a falling out with one another and neither of you has been willing to settle your differences, your child has a serious drug or alcohol problem and you are concerned that any assets you leave to him or her will be used to feed that addiction, your child hasn't communicated with you in a long time, and so on. Sometimes, however, parents leave a child out of their estate plan, not because they're unhappy with the child, but because they've decided that the child doesn't need any of their assets.

Whatever your reasons for disinheriting one of your children, don't do it until you've considered all of the possible consequences of making that move, not just for the child you want to disinherit, but for his or her siblings, too. For example, it's possible that:

■ The child you disinherit will forever believe that you didn't love him or her.
■ The disinheritance may create tension and bad feelings between that child and your other children who did inherit from you. For example, they may disagree with one another about whether their sibling should have been disinherited or about whether they have an obligation to help that sibling out because of what you've done.
■ The child you disinherit will become a financial burden for your other children.
■ The child you disinherit will try to contest your will or living trust.
■ The children of the child you've disinherited might be ostracized by your other grandchildren or feel ashamed.
■ Your child might respond to your decision by becoming self-destructive.

Given all of these possible consequences, here are some alternatives to disinheriting a child that you may want to consider:

■ Repair your broken relationship with your child.
■ Make your child the beneficiary of an incentive trust, as described earlier in this chapter.
■ Leave your child a small amount of money in trust or as an outright gift, together with an explanation for what you are doing and maybe some words

Disagreements over your estate plan can cause irreparable damage to your children's relationships with one another.

of love and forgiveness, or even an apology, if appropriate.

If you do decide to disinherit your child, your will or trust should be very clear about what you are doing and why. Otherwise, the child might try to contest what you've done by claiming that you actually intended to include him or her in your plan but forgot to. To minimize the likelihood of a contest, your attorney may also advise that you make your intentions extra clear by having you videotaped while signing your will or living trust document and answering questions about your decision on camera. It's also a good idea to let your child know what you have done in person, by phone, or through a letter. It's possible that after hearing from you, your child may decide to change his or her ways as a result, and the two of you may reach a rapprochement. As a result, you may decide to include that child in your estate plan after all.

Keeping the Peace in Your Family

Most us of have heard horror stories about adult children who battled with one another over their parent's estate. The battles may have been sparked by the children's unmet expectations about how much they would inherit, the terms and conditions of their inheritance, or because some of them were angry and resentful that assets they wanted went to their siblings. Sadly, research shows that as baby boomers move closer to retirement age and become increasingly concerned about how they are going to fund their golden years, the incidence of inheritance-related family feuds is growing.

Disagreements over your estate plan can cause irreparable damage to your children's relationships with one another. In addition, if any of your children are really upset, they may contest your will or living trust to try to undo the provisions that bother them. You cannot totally eliminate the potential for bickering and fighting among your children after your death, but you can take some actions now to minimize the potential for discord later. For example, you can:

■ Discuss your estate plan with your children, and answer any questions they may have about it. Talking with them may even highlight flaws in your planning that would never have occurred to you otherwise, and as a result, you might decide to revise your plan.

■ Write a letter to all of your children or an individual letter to each one that explains the values, issues, and considerations that you took into account when you were preparing your plan. Give the letter(s) to the executor of your will or the trustee of their trust(s).

■ Create a video for your children, to be viewed immediately after your death, that explains your estate plan to them.

■ Discuss your concerns with your estate planning attorney. He or she may have other suggestions.

Also, as discussed in Chapter 2, the "small stuff" in your estate—items you wouldn't ordinarily include in your will or through your living trust, like your old sports trophies, the family Bible, that silly knickknack that has sat on the shelf in your den for years, a framed photo of you and your spouse on your wedding day, or a jar full of old buttons—may have tremendous emotional value to your children. In fact, it's not uncommon for these kinds of items to provoke heated battles among children when a parent dies without deciding ahead of time which child will get what or without establishing a system for their children to divvy everything up.

This chapter laid out your estate planning options when it comes to your minor and adult children. It highlighted the pros and cons of each option as well as many of the issues you may want to take into account when you are planning for your children. The chapter also told you about some of the specific types of trusts you can use to provide for your kids, discussed disinheriting a child, and provided tips for minimizing the likelihood that your adult children will come into conflict with one another over your estate plan after your death.

When You Can No Longer Make Decisions

Part 4

Planning for Your Finances and Health Care in Case You Become Incapacitated

Although most of us associate estate planning with planning for our deaths, estate planning also involves planning for the possibility that we may become temporarily or permanently incapacitated. This may occur because of an injury or illness, and as a result, you will be unable to manage your own finances or make your own health care decisions. Not addressing these possibilities now, by legally designating who you want to manage your finances and who you want to make health care decisions on your behalf, can have serious negative financial and emotional consequences for you and your loved ones if you do become incapacitated.

Controlling Your Finances If You Become Incapacitated

Who will mange your finances and your business interests if you become incompetent and you can't manage them yourself? Who will take care of your banking, file your income tax returns, and manage your stock portfolio? Who will run your small business and handle your rental properties? If you own all of your assets with your spouse and if you have a business partner, those people should be able to handle some aspects of your financial and business life if you can't. However, what if your signature is needed on a document to complete a financial transaction or if the assets in your investment portfolio need reallocating to maintain the portfolio's value? What if you need to implement some aspect of your estate plan, like transferring some of your individual assets to your living trust or amending your will? Also, what if your spouse divorces you after you become incompetent or your business partner decides to exit your business? What if you don't have a spouse or a business partner?

It's because of these kinds of eventualities, and many more, that it's an essential part of your estate planning to legally designate the person you want to manage your financial and business affairs if you become incompetent. However, if you decide to transfer all of your assets to a living trust, then the trustee of the trust can mange them for you if you become incapacitated.

Durable Power of Attorney

In order to designate an individual that will be responsible for managing your finances in the event that you're unable to, you must prepare a legal document called a *durable power of attorney* for your finances. The person you name in that document will be referred to as your *financial agent*, also called an *attorney-in-fact* or *surrogate*. A durable power of attorney can help you ensure that your assets will be well managed in the event of your incapacitation. It can also help preserve the value of your estate so that it will be available to help meet the needs of you and your family while you are alive and so that as much of your estate as possible will pass to your loved ones when you die.

If you are working with an estate planning attorney, he or she will prepare your power of attorney document. However, you can also prepare your own using a generic fill-in-the-blanks form that you purchase at an office supply store, or you can create one online at a legal website such as Legacy.com (*www.legacy.com*) or LawDepot (*www.lawdepot.com*).

Be sure that you prepare a *durable* power of attorney document, however, not a document that is *limited*. Here's why: When you give someone a limited power of attorney, his or her power to act on your behalf is automatically cancelled as soon as a doctor certifies that you are legally incompetent—just when you need help the most. That's not the case when the power of attorney is durable. Also, make sure that the form will be legally valid in your state.

Deciding What Responsibilities You'll Give to Your Financial Agent

Generally, if you prepare your power of attorney, the powers that you give to your financial agent will be broadly stated without any terms or conditions. They will probably include the power to buy, sell, manage, and borrow against any and every kind of property that you own and the power to enter into real estate transactions of any and all types, among other general powers.

If your attorney prepares the document for you, however, you can customize it to meet your needs. For example, you may or may not want to give your financial agent the right to:

- Handle all of your banking, including paying your bills, managing your bank accounts, opening new accounts in your name, and opening and closing bank-card accounts (MasterCard and Visa accounts).

- Make all expenditures necessary to maintain the standard of living you and your family currently enjoy.
- Manage and sell your real estate and buy real estate on your behalf.
- Buy and sell stocks, bonds, mutual funds, and commodities, and exercise options on your behalf.
- File insurance claims on your behalf, purchase insurance in your name, and terminate policies.
- Buy, sell, and manage your personal property.
- Manage all benefits (government and private) that you currently receive, and apply for all benefits to which you are entitled. Possible benefits include Social Security and veteran's benefits, Supplemental Security Income benefits, Medicare and Medicaid benefits, and employer retirement benefits. Also, your property may be transferred as necessary to make sure that you qualify for all medical assistance programs.
- Manage your business interests.
- Handle all litigation including filing lawsuits, defending you and your estate against lawsuits, and settling lawsuits on your behalf.
- Manage your tax obligations, including filing tax returns, collecting refunds, and negotiating with the IRS.
- Make inter vivos gifts of your property.
- Implement your estate plan, including the power to change the beneficiary for your life insurance policy, execute a will or codicil in your name, amend a trust that you've set up, and so on.
- Continue to support the charities that you have supported in the past.
- Hire professionals to care for you or for your family members.
- Do anything that you would do if you could manage your own finances.

A power of attorney that is legally enforceable in one state will usually be recognized by another state. So if you own property in more than one state, your document should apply to the assets that are located outside your state of residence. It should also apply if you move to a new state. To be absolutely sure, however, talk to an estate planning attorney.

Choosing Your Financial Agent

Obviously, given that you will be entrusting your financial life and well-being (and your family's, too) to your financial agent, the person you choose to serve in that capacity should be someone that you trust completely. It should be someone who does a good job managing his or her own finances and who will have the time to manage your affairs as well. Also, if your financial agent will be managing relatively complex assets such as rental property; a portfolio of stocks, bonds, and mutual funds; or your business interests, it's a good idea if that person has actual hands-on experience managing those kinds of assets. Otherwise, your financial agent may have to learn how to manage them "on the job" by making mistakes with your assets.

Though most people choose a family member or close friend as their financial agent, if no one you know fits the bill, then you'll need to consider your attorney, banker, financial advisor, CPA, or some other professional. However, keep in mind that although a friend of family member may not expect to be paid for managing your finances, a financial professional will. A professional will probably bill your estate on an hourly basis or charge it a fee based on the value of the assets he or she is managing. Even so, the cost of professional help will probably be a small price to pay for the peace of mind you will gain knowing that your financial and business affairs won't disintegrate, and the value of your estate will be preserved.

Designating Co-agents to Handle Your Finances

Rather than designating one person to act as your financial agent, you can designate co-agents. This might be a good arrangement if your first choice for a financial agent is out of the country a lot and you want someone to act as his or her backup on an as-needed basis. Co-agents are helpful if you don't know any one person who has all of the financial and business management skills you are looking for. If you decide to appoint co-agents, you should hire an estate planning attorney to draw up your power of attorney document so that the responsibilities of each co-agent will be clearly defined, in order to minimize the potential for problems. Be sure to appoint at least one alternate financial agent for each of your designees, although two alternates per designee is best.

Once Your Document Is Drafted

If you prepare your own power of attorney document, it's a good idea to pay an estate planning attorney to review it, so you can be absolutely sure that it will be legally enforceable and that it will adequately protect you and your family if it's activated. It should take an attorney about an hour to review it.

You should also review the document with whomever you want to serve as your financial agent and with your choice for an alternate, too. It's critical that they completely understand what you expect of them and that they feel comfortable with your expectations and confident that they can carry out your wishes. These conversations will also give your designees an opportunity to ask you questions about your finances, find out where your important documents are stored, and so on.

Once your document has been finalized, sign it and have it witnessed in accordance with your state's law. Don't forget to get it notarized if that's a requirement in your state. Give a copy of the document to your financial agent and the alternate, and store the original with the rest of your estate planning documents. You may also want to give a copy to your spouse or partner and to the financial professionals with whom you work.

Whenever you review your estate plan, review your durable power of attorney for finances, too. Make sure that it continues to reflect the realities of your finances and business affairs and that you are still comfortable with whomever you have chosen as your financial agent and alternate, as well as with the powers that you have given to them. If you want to change anything or cancel the power of attorney, get back all copies, destroy them along with the original, and prepare a new power of attorney.

Whenever you review your estate plan, review your durable power of attorney for finances, too.

If You Become Incapacitated without a Financial Agent

Nothing may happen at first if you become temporarily or permanently incapacitated and you haven't given someone the right to manage your financial and business affairs. Eventually, however, one of your family members, your business partner, or someone else will probably file a legal petition with the probate court in your area, formally asking it to appoint a *guardian* (called a *conservator* in some states) to mange your financial or business affairs. Then a court hearing, which will be open to the public, will be scheduled so that a probate judge can confirm that you are incompetent, and then decide who will be your guardian.

The court will notify all of your legal heirs and anyone else who may have a legal stake in the court's decision about the hearing so that they may attend. Some of them may hire attorneys to represent their interests. The judge will also appoint an attorney to represent you. Your estate will pay the attorney's fees and expenses, which may be substantial.

People who know you may have to testify at the hearing, including your family members and friends, business associates, spiritual advisor, and others. Professional experts may be called to testify as well, such as doctors, mental health professionals, financial experts, and so on. If your attorney calls any experts to testify on your behalf, your estate will also pay their fees and expenses.

The guardianship hearing may be emotionally difficult for your loved ones, especially if embarrassing or painful information is presented as evidence. If your loved ones are divided about who should be put in charge of your finances, they may air their disagreements in the courtroom.

The judge will appoint a guardian for you if he or she concludes that you are incompetent. Although your guardian may be someone you know like your spouse or partner, one of your adult children, one of your siblings, or one of your personal advisors, there is no guarantee that whoever is appointed will be the same person you would have chosen to have power of attorney for your finances. It's also possible that the judge will appoint a financial professional who is a stranger to you and to your family members.

What's Wrong with a Guardianship?

There's a lot wrong with a guardianship. For example:

- Your guardian will be required to maintain detailed records about your finances and business affairs. He or she will have to provide the court with regular reports regarding the status of your affairs, which helps to protect you, but all of that information will be available to the public.

- Your guardian will have to get the court's permission to take certain actions on your behalf, like selling your real estate, for example, and the court's permission process will be slow and cumbersome. The delays could have a negative effect on your estate, be inconvenient for your family, and maybe even create financial problems for them.

- Your guardian will be entitled to receive a court-determined fee for his or her services, which will be paid for by your estate. Your estate will also have to pay the cost of your guardian's bond and the fees and expenses of any professionals he or she may have to hire. Obviously, the longer your guardianship lasts, the more of your estate these fees and expenses will eat up.

- Some of your family members may contest the need for a guardianship or may formally object to whoever is named as your guardian. If that happens, there will be more public hearings and more fees and expenses for your estate to pay.

- The judge may unknowingly appoint someone whose decisions about your finances are motivated by greed and self-interest, not by what's in the best interest of you and your family, and your estate may be harmed as a result. Although the court's reporting requirements are intended to protect you from such a possibility,

To control your health care should you become incapacitated, you must prepare what are generally referred to as advance medical directives.

they assume that the court will carefully read your guardian's reports and scrutinize his or her records in a timely manner, and usually that's not what happens.

Your guardianship will end when one of three things happens: You are no longer incompetent, you die, or all of the assets in your estate are used up, and nothing is left for your guardian to manage. If your guardian resigns from the job, the judge will appoint someone else to manage your affairs.

Controlling Your Health Care If You Become Incapacitated

Right now, you make your own medical decisions and decide how you want to spend your health care dollars. But unless you prepare the appropriate documents, directing your own medical care will be impossible if you become incapacitated by a stroke, Alzheimer's, a coma, or some other serious medical problem affecting your brain. Instead, someone else—maybe your doctor, a family member, or someone who is appointed by the court—will make medical decisions for you, and their decisions may not mirror the ones you would make if you were able. Furthermore, their decisions may have a dramatic impact on both your quality of life and the dignity with which you live out your remaining time—and they may eat up your estate to boot. Thus, careful planning regarding who will make medical decisions on your behalf in the event you become unable to do so is crucial.

Advance Medical Directives

To control your health care should you become incapacitated, you must prepare what are generally referred to as *advance medical directives*. These legal documents are a critically important part of any estate plan. One kind of directive is called a *durable medical power of attorney*. The purpose of this document is to designate the person who will act as your *health care agent* when one or more medical doctors (the exact number depends on your state) certify that you're not competent to make your own medical decisions. The document will also give your health care agent the right to make specific kinds of health care decisions on your behalf. The other kind of advance medical directive is a living will, which spells out the kinds of medical care you do and don't want to receive at the end of your life. Some states combine both kinds of directives into one document.

Advance directives are not just for elderly people or people who are hospitalized or suffering from a serious illness. Anyone at any age can become critically injured in an accident or critically ill and unable to direct their own health care. Regardless of your current age or health, if you care who will make your health care decisions when you can't make them for yourself, then advance directives must be a part of your estate plan.

Preparing Your Advance Medical Directives

If an estate planning attorney prepares your estate plan, he or she will help you create your advance medical directives. However, you can prepare your own using standardized forms that you may obtain from a hospital in your area, from your primary care doctor, or from your local agency on aging. You may also find them online at websites such as Compassion & Choices (*www.compassionandchoices.org*) and LegacyWriter (*www. legacywriter.com*). When you visit these sites, you will be asked to select your state of residence because different states require different forms. If you spend a lot of time in another state, prepare advance directives for that other state too, because some states will only honor advance directives that meet their particular standards.

The standard forms will come with instructions explaining how to make them legally binding, including the number of adults who must witness you signing your completed documents—most states require two witnesses—and whether you must get the documents notarized. The instructions will also tell you who *can't* be a witness. Usually that includes anyone who is a beneficiary of your estate plan or who would inherit from you according to your state's intestacy law.

The standard forms in some states automatically give your health care agent broad decision-making authority. This may include the right to approve or refuse certain kinds of treatments, the right to arrange medical services for you (including the right to admit you to a hospital or nursing home), and the right to pay for your care using your funds. Many state forms also automatically give your health care agent the right to make decisions about your end-of-life care, such as the right to end or withhold treatment so that you may die naturally. The forms in other states, however, allow you to specifically indicate the kinds of care and treatment you do and don't want. Also, most forms let you indicate whether you want your organs donated for transplantation or for medical research.

Drawbacks to Using Standard Advance Directive Forms

The primary drawback to using generic forms to create your standard advance directives is that the forms only address a rather narrowly defined set of medical-related issues, and the powers that you give to your health care agent are stated in black and white. In other words, you usually have no means of attaching terms or conditions to those powers like, "I only want to receive blood transfusions, if..." or "I only want to be tube fed when..." or other directives that are not listed on the form. However, you can create legally binding advance medical directives that are more detailed and specific.

Going beyond the Usual with a Letter of Instruction

In addition to preparing advance directives, you may want to a write a letter of instruction to your health care agent to help make your wishes absolutely clear and to provide any additional information that can help guide his or her decision making when the time comes. For example, in your letter you may want to discuss:

- The current state of your health.
- What you consider to be a good quality of life and what, in your opinion, would represent an undesirable quality of life.
- Your attitude toward pain.
- Under what conditions you would want specific treatments or procedures like kidney dialysis, tube feeding, being put on a ventilator, being given certain kinds of drugs, and so on.
- Your attitudes toward death and dying.
- Who you do or don't want to visit you in a hospital or a nursing home.
- The religious beliefs and values that are the underpinnings of the wishes you've expressed in your durable medical power of attorney document and your living will.
- Whether you want to die at home.

- Whether you want hospice care.
- Who you would like by your side when you die.
- Whether you want your body autopsied.
- Your burial wishes.

When you complete your letter of instruction, be sure to attach it to your advance medical directives.

Customizing your advance directives and writing a letter of instruction are especially good ideas if you are concerned that one of your family members may try to prevent your health care agent from carrying out your wishes. Documents that explicitly state the exact powers you are giving to your health care agent, which are clear about the rationale behind your wishes, will help bolster your agent's decision-making authority should it be challenged.

Choosing Your Health Care Agent

The person you choose as your health care agent should be someone you trust implicitly given the important life-and-death decisions you will be placing in his or her hands. Among other qualities, your health care agent should be comfortable talking with doctors and nurses and standing up to them on your behalf when necessary. He or she should share your values and views on medical care in general and on end-of-life care in particular.

Don't choose someone as your health care agent who tends to crumble under stress, isn't good at handling emotionally difficult matters, or in poor health. Don't choose someone who is easily manipulated, indecisive, or too emotionally close to you to make tough decisions on your behalf when the time comes. Also, steer clear of anyone who you think might let his or her inheritance from you influence decisions about your medical care.

It may be hard for you to imagine that such a thing could happen. But any estate planning attorney can tell you stories of seemingly upstanding, trustworthy people who became greedy and calculating in such situations. They may have been charged with managing the medical care of someone else and stood to benefit financially if they made certain decisions like withholding care, opting for less expensive care, and so on.

Depending on your state, you may be prohibited from designating certain people as your health care agent. These people may include your health care provider, any of your health care provider's employees, your residential care provider, and any of that provider's employees.

If you are in a same-sex relationship, you may want to appoint your partner as your health care agent to ensure that if you become incapacitated, the doctors will consult with him or her about your medical care and about end-of-life issues. Doing this is especially important if your state has no law that requires such consultation and if your family doesn't approve of your relationship. In fact, in most states, unless you give your partner a durable power of attorney for your medical care, he or she will not be entitled to visit you in your hospital room when you are critically ill or injured.

After you have drafted your advance medical directives and your letter of instruction, review everything with whomever you are asking to be your health care agent and your alternate. Make sure both individuals understand your wishes and are clear about the moral values, religious beliefs, and considerations that you may have taken into account when you prepared the documents. If either of them is at all uncomfortable with your wishes, ask someone else to be your health care agent or alternate.

Communicate Your Wishes

Once your advance medical directives are finalized and you have finished your letter of instruction, review them with:

■ **Your immediate family.** If they are uncomfortable with any of your wishes and/or with whomever you have chosen as your health care agent and alternate, do what you can to help them understand your thinking. Ideally, even if your choices aren't what they would choose for themselves, they will support your right to make them.

■ **Your doctor.** If your doctor is uncomfortable with any of your choices or indicates that he or she won't help get your living will activated should that time come, you probably want to find a new doctor.

After your advance medical directives have been properly executed, give a copy of each document to your health care agent, your primary care doctor, your spouse or partner, and anyone else who needs one. Also, make sure that your health care agent knows that if you are moved to a nursing home or if you are hospitalized, he or she should provide the facility with copies, too. Store your original documents with the rest of your estate planning documents and make sure that your health care agent and at least one other person knows where they are stored and how to access them.

It's also a good idea to carry a card or a handwritten note in your wallet stating that you have prepared advance medical directives and providing the name and contact information for your health care agent. That way, if you are alone when you become ill or injured, whoever is caring for you will have this information if you can't convey it yourself.

Periodically, review your advance medical directives along with the rest of your estate plan so that you can be sure that they continue to reflect your wishes. If you want to change anything, get back all copies of whatever document you want to change, destroy them, and prepare a new one. Then make copies for all of the appropriate people.

Controlling the End of Your Life with a Living Will

In our medically advanced society, life-sustaining medical care like tube feeding and hydration can keep you alive for months, if not years, when you are terminally ill, injured, or in a persistent vegetative state. However, a living will gives you a say about the kinds of end-of-life care you do and don't want when you are close to death.

When you prepare your living will, you will have to make decisions about such matters as whether you want to:

- Be resuscitated if your heart stops.
- Be kept alive through artificial feeding and/or hydration.
- Be kept alive with a respirator or mechanical ventilator.
- Receive blood transfusions.
- Be kept pain-free.
- Receive chemotherapy, radiation treatment, or kidney dialysis.
- Receive an organ transplant.
- Be operated on surgically.
- Receive antibiotics and/or pain medication.

The Benefits of Having a Living Will

Besides giving you control over your end-of-life care and the opportunity to die with dignity, writing a living will also provides other benefits.

Besides giving you control over your end-of-life care and the opportunity to die with dignity, writing a living will also provides other benefits.

It helps you ensure that your estate will not be depleted by the cost of care that you may not want. We're not telling you anything you don't already know—even with good insurance, aggressive end-of-life medical care and treatment is costly—which means that after you die, there could be a lot less of your estate for your loved ones.

It spares your family from having to make emotionally difficult life-and-death decisions on your behalf, maybe without any idea about what you would want. When you are dying and you have no living will, the doctors in charge of your medical care will use their own judgment about the medications and treatments you should receive day to day. Because the focus of their medical training is on saving lives, they will try to keep you alive as long as possible. However, your doctors will consult with your immediate family members about what to do if you need surgery, an organ transplant, dialysis, chemotherapy, or some other major medical procedure or treatment. As we've already warned in this chapter, the decisions your family members make may not mirror what you would choose if you had written a living will. For example, your family's religious values may dictate that everything possible be done to sustain your life, but your values may be totally different. Furthermore, fear, grief, or an inability to let go and allow nature to take its course may interfere with their decision making. In most states, doctors are not legally obligated to consult with a patient's same-sex partner.

It minimizes the likelihood that there will be disagreements within your family about what to

do, which often happens when families are under stress. The highly publicized Terry Schiavo case dramatically demonstrated just how bad things can get. Schiavo was the young, brain-dead Florida woman whose spouse and parents were locked in an emotionally charged, highly public battle about whether she should be allowed to die by removing her feeding tube.

Appointing a Guardian for Your Health Care

If your family can't resolve their own disagreements, the court will get involved. At some point either the hospital that's caring for you or one of your family members will probably ask the court to appoint someone to act as your guardian. This person will have the right to make medical decisions on your behalf, under the court's supervision.

Before a guardian can be appointed, however, there will be a guardianship hearing, which will be open to the public. During the hearing there will be testimony about your medical condition and about who should be named as your guardian. Some of the testimony may be difficult for your family members to hear, and some of your family members may have to testify, as well. In addition, the guardianship proceeding will cost your estate money because the court will need to appoint an attorney to represent your interests during the hearing, and your estate will pay the attorney's fees and expenses. Also, if your attorney calls any experts to testify on your behalf, your estate will pay their fees and expenses, too. Once a guardian has been appointed to direct your medical care, he or she will be entitled to receive a fee for the duration of the guardianship, and your estate will pay that, as well.

Your living will is a highly personal document, so it should be a reflection of your values and beliefs, not what someone else thinks.

Some Other Things to Consider When You Are Preparing Your Living Will

Here are a few other things you should know about living wills.

- When you are preparing your living will, you may want to consult with your doctor if you are unsure about the exact purpose of certain medical procedures or if you want to better understand when they might be appropriate. You may also want to talk things over with your religious advisor.

- When you prepare your living will, it will be impossible to address every possible situation that might arise. Therefore, the wishes you express in it will serve as a guide for your health care agent. In the end, you'll have to trust that person to make the right decisions for you.

- It's possible that your living will may not be immediately available when you are near death. In fact, several studies indicate that this is the case about 75 percent of the time. For example, your loved ones or the doctors who are caring for you may not know that you have a living will, or they may not know where your living will is stored. One way to make certain that your living will is available when it's needed is to register it with a living will registry like DocuBank (*www.docubank.com*) or U.S. Living Will Registry (*www. uslivingwillregistry.com*). When you do, you'll receive a card to carry in your wallet that says you have a living will and that provides a phone number and email address that medical personnel can use 24/7 to have your living will emailed or faxed to them.

- Your living will is a highly personal document, so it should be a reflection of your values and beliefs, not what someone else thinks. Therefore, never let any-one influence what you put in your living will.

Activating Your Living Will

Your health care agent will not determine when your living will can be activated. The living will laws of your state make that determination. Most of those laws say that a living will cannot be activated unless two doctors certify in writing that you're not competent to make your own health care decisions and that you are terminally ill or injured or in a permanent vegetative state. Despite what the law says, however, getting a living will activated is often easier said than done. For example:

- There may be questions about the validity of your living will.
- The doctors who are caring for you may disagree about whether your medical condition meets your state's activation criteria, or they may have moral or religious objections to living wills and may not be anxious to activate yours.
- One of your immediate family members may put a lot of pressure on your doctors not to activate your living will.

In the face of such roadblocks, your health care agent will have to push to get your living will activated. He or she may do that by talking with the doctors who are in charge of your care, speaking with your family members, meeting with hospital administrators, or getting the court involved.

This chapter stressed the importance of planning for the possibility that you may become incapacitated at some point and unable to direct your own financial and business affairs and health care decisions. As part of your estate planning, you should designate a financial agent and a health care agent to mange your finances and your medical care. You should prepare a durable power of attorney for your finances and a durable medical power of attorney. The advice provided for choosing your financial and health care agents, along with what kinds of powers you may want to give them, should get you on the right track. In addition, the benefits of controlling your end-of-life care with a living will, as well as the issues you should consider when you write yours, should now be clear. This should help you determine the kinds of provisions you may want to include when preparing your living will.

ow that you've read this book, you should have a good understanding of everything that is involved in estate planning. Among other things, *Kiplinger's Estate Planning* has informed you about:

- Why you need an estate plan, and what will happen if you die without one.
- What you can accomplish with your estate plan, including determining who will inherit your assets when you die, helping to preserve the value of your estate by having the right kinds of insurance, implementing estate tax minimization strategies when appropriate, and planning for your possible incapacitation.
- The pros and cons of building your estate plan on a will versus a living trust, as well as why you still need a will if you opt for a living trust.
- Other estate planning tools besides wills and living trusts that you can use to pass on your assets to your loved ones when you die, including life insurance, retirement accounts, custodial accounts, and inter vivos gifts.
- How the federal gift and estate taxes work, how much your estate must be worth in order to owe estate taxes when you die, and strategies for reducing the amount of those taxes.
- The value of preparing your estate plan with the help of an estate planning attorney, and the various types

You'll rest easier once you have a plan in place, knowing that you've done everything you can to secure your family's future financial well-being.

of do-it-yourself estate plan resources, including their benefits and risks.

- Other personal finance professionals you should involve in your estate planning.
- The different kinds of trusts you can set up through your will or through your living trust in order to achieve specific estate planning goals.
- The special kinds of estate planning decisions you must make when you are the parent of minor children.
- The options you have for including your spouse or unmarried partner and your young or adult children in your estate plan.
- The estate planning challenges faced by same-sex partners.
- The importance of keeping your estate planning documents up-to-date by reviewing them regularly and revising them as necessary.
- The probate process, the role of an executor in that process, and how to choose an executor to guide your estate through probate.
- Using an ethical will to convey your personal legacy to your loved ones.

With the information in this book and the assistance of a good estate planning attorney, you are well equipped to craft a plan that meets your estate planning goals and reflects the realities of your finances and your family situation. You'll rest easier once you have a plan in place, knowing that you've done everything you can to secure your family's future financial well-being. And you'll have minimized the likelihood that their lives will be filled with legal hassles and expenses, stress, and emotional upset after your death and/or your incapacitation.

For the latest information on estate planning or to find out more about a specific estate planning subject in this book, be sure to read *Kiplinger's Personal Finance Magazine* and to visit the magazine's website, *www.kiplinger.com*.

This book would not be possible without the help of so many people, and I want to thank as many of them as I can. First, I want to thank my writing partner and closest friend, Mary Reed. I don't think I would have been as successful an author without our partnership. I also want to thank Professor Ira Shepard of the University of Houston Law School, who helped me simplify complex estate planning concepts, and attorney Keith Morris, who specializes in estate planning and who gave this book a thorough read through and added his valuable suggestions. Finally, I want to thank my editors at Kaplan Publishing, Shannon Berning and Eric Titner, both of whom were a pleasure to work with.

Acknowledgments

A trust: The surviving spouse's portion of an A/B trust. It's also called a marital trust, among other things.

Abatement: The forced reduction of the gifts in your will when there are not enough assets in your probate estate to pay all of your estate's administrative expenses, debts, and gifts or bequests.

A/B trust: A trust that allows both spouses to take advantage of their individual federal estate tax exemptions, so that both of them can transfer their assets without owing any estate taxes.

Administration: The court-supervised management of your estate after your death, including the distribution of the assets in your estate when you die without an estate plan.

Administrator: The person the probate court will appoint to administer your estate during the probate process if you die without an estate plan. An administrator has the same responsibilities as an executor.

Annual exclusion: The total amount that you can give to as many people as you want every year while you are alive without incurring a gift or estate tax. At the time this book was written, that amount was $12,000 per person. However, in 2009 it is expected to increase to $13,000 per person.

Assets: The property you own, including your real property and your personal property—your bank accounts, brokerage accounts, life insurance, furniture, jewelry, collectibles, clothing, and so on.

Attorney-in-fact: The person you designate in a power of attorney document to perform specific activities on your behalf. For example, as a part of your estate planning, you should give someone the power to manage your financial affairs and your medical care if you become mentally incapacitated.

Beneficiary: An individual or an organization who will benefit from your will or living trust. The beneficiary may be someone you know, a charity, or a college or university. You also designate a beneficiary when you purchase life insurance, open a retirement account, and so on.

Bequest: A gift of personal property that you leave to someone in your will. Your personal property may include stocks and bonds, jewelry, artwork, your vehicle, books, clothing, and so on. It dos not include real estate.

Bond: A guarantee provided by a bonding company that if the individual or business to whom it sold the bond fails to perform appropriately specific duties and anyone is damaged (harmed) as a result, the injured party will be compensated. Executors, trustees, and property guardians are often bonded.

B trust: The deceased's portion of an A/B trust. It's also called a bypass or credit shelter trust, among other things.

Bypass trust: Another name for the B part of an A/B trust.

Charitable lead trust: A kind of trust that pays income generated by the trust assets to a charity for a certain number of years. When those years are up, whatever is left in the trust passes to the trust's beneficiaries, who are usually the family members of the trust maker.

Charitable remainder trust: A kind of trust that pays income to the trust maker for the rest of his or her life; whatever is left in the trust when the trust maker dies passes to the charity designated in the trust agreement.

Children's trust: A trust that is created for minor children.

Codicil: A formal legal document amending a will. An appropriately drafted and executed codicil is as legally enforceable as a will and considered part of a will.

Community property: Income earned and property acquired by married couples in the states of Arizona, California, Idaho, Louisiana, Nevada, New Mexico, Texas, Washington, and Wisconsin. Each spouse owns a one-half interest in those assets. Inheritances and gifts received by one spouse during a marriage are not treated as community property. Couples in community property states can only transfer their one-half share of their community property through their estate plans.

Conservator: An adult who is legally responsible for the care and well-being of another adult. This person is called a guardian in some states.

Contest: To challenge the legal validity of a will or a trust.

Cotrustees: Two or more people who are responsible for the joint management of a trust.

Credit shelter trust: Another name for a bypass trust or a B trust.

Custodian: The person in charge of the assets in a custodial account set up for a minor child under the Uniform Gifts to Minors Act or the Uniform Transfers to Minors Act.

Death taxes: Another term used for estate taxes.

Disinherit: To leave a legal heir out of your estate plan. The term is most often associated with spouses and children.

Durable power of attorney for finances: A legal document designating the person you want to manage your finances—your financial agent—if you become incapacitated, which specifies the powers and responsibilities you are giving to this person. (*See also* Power of attorney.)

Estate: All of the assets that you own. An estate can be divided into several sub-estates—the assets in your probate estate and the assets in your taxable estate.

Estate planning: The process of planning for the orderly transfer of your assets before and after your death, or for the management of your assets and your medical care in the event that you become incapacitated. Estate planning also involves preserving your wealth, which includes minimizing the amount of taxes your estate may owe at your death.

Estate taxes: The taxes your estate will owe if it is worth more than a certain amount. There are federal estate taxes, and some states have their own estate taxes. Also called an inheritance or a death tax.

Executor: The person or financial institution that you name in your will to carry out the instructions in your will after your death. Your executor will pay any debts and estate taxes you may owe, and make certain that your wishes are carried out during the probate process, among other things.

Funding: Transferring assets to a trust.

Gift: Any property that you voluntarily give to someone else free of charge while you are alive.

Gift tax: A federal tax your estate may owe if you give someone more than the federal annual gift exclusion amount. At the time that this book was written, a gift tax is owed if you give someone more than $12,000 annually. You also have a lifetime gift tax exclusion, which was $1 million when this book was written. If the total value of the inter vivos gifts you make while you're alive exceeds this amount, your estate will owe a gift tax on the excess when you die.

Gift tax exclusion: The amount of a gift that is not subject to a gift tax, normally expressed on an annual basis. (*See also* Gift tax.) You also have a lifetime gift tax exclusion. It was $1 million as of this book's printing.

Grantor: The person who creates a trust. Also called a trust maker, trustor, donor, or settlor.

Heir: Someone who is legally entitled to inherit from you according to the inheritance laws of your state, when you die without having written a will or transferred your assets to a living trust.

Holographic will: A handwritten will. Most states do not consider this kind of will to be legally valid.

Inter vivos gift: An asset that you give away while you are alive. Once you give it way, you cannot retain any interest in the asset, nor can you maintain any control over it. People often make inter vivos gifts to reduce the size of their taxable estates.

Inter vivos trust: A kind of trust that you establish while you are alive, also called a living trust. It may be revocable or irrevocable.

Intestate: Dying without a will or without having transferred your assets to a living trust.

Irrevocable life insurance trust: A trust set up to hold a life insurance policy in order to remove the policy from your taxable estate.

Joint property: Assets owned by more than one person.

Joint tenancy assets: Assets that are owned equally by at least two people. When one owner dies, his or her share of a joint tenancy asset transfers automatically to the other owner(s). Married and unmarried couples often own assets this way. Also referred to as joint assets.

Joint will: A will that is shared by two people—usually a married couple. This is not recommended.

Living trust: A kind of trust that you establish while you are alive. It may be revocable or irrevocable. Also called an inter vivos trust.

Living will: A legally binding document that states the kinds of life-sustaining care and treatment you do and don't want to receive when you are terminally ill or injured.

Marital deduction: A federal tax deduction that allows one spouse to leave the other spouse all of his or her assets estate tax–free, regardless of their value.

Minor child: A child who is younger than 18 or 21, depending on the child's state of residence.

Net taxable estate: The value of your estate when you die less all of your estate's liabilities, administrative expenses, and any applicable deductions.

Payable-on-death account: A bank account that holds money for the future benefit of whomever you've designated as the account beneficiary. The beneficiary will receive those funds when you die. Also called a Totten trust or informal trust.

Personal guardian: An adult whom you designate in your will as the person who will raise your children should you die while they are minors and should their other parent also be deceased or unable/unwilling to raise them.

Personal property: All of the property that you own other than your real estate (your home or condo, rental property, other buildings, and undeveloped land).

Pour-over will: A will that transfers to your living trust any assets that you did not transfer to the trust before you died.

Power of attorney: A legal document that gives another adult the legal authority to act on your behalf and that spells out the specific powers you are (or are not) giving to that adult, who is referred to as your *attorney in fact* or *legal agent*. The powers may be very broad or very narrow, and they may be durable or limited. If they are durable, the powers of your legal agent do not end if you become incapacitated and unable to manage your own affairs. (*See also* Durable power of attorney for finances.)

Probate: The state court process that determines the legal validity of your will, authorizes your executor to pay any debts and taxes your estate may owe, and pays all of your estate's administrative expenses. It also distributes your assets either to the beneficiaries you've designated in your will or to your legal heirs if you died without a will (and you did not transfer all of your assets to a living trust). During probate, the court also formally appoints your executor or an administrator for your estate.

Probate estate: The assets you own that go through probate.

Property guardian: The adult or institution you name in your will to manage the assets that you leave to your minor children in your will.

Real property: Your home or condo, rental property, other buildings, and undeveloped land.

Residuary beneficiary: Whoever gets the assets in your estate that you have not left to a specific beneficiary after all creditor claims, taxes, and probate-related administrative expenses have been paid.

Residuary estate: The assets that remain in your estate after all of your debts, expenses, and taxes have been paid and all assets that you left to specific beneficiaries in your will have been transferred. The assets may pass to the residuary beneficiary of your will or they may be transferred via your pour-over will to your living trust.

Revocable trust: A trust that can be changed or revoked.

Right of survivorship: When two people own an asset as joint tenants (or as tenants in the entirety), the right of the surviving owner to the deceased's share of the asset. That share will transfer automatically. More than two people can be joint tenants.

Separate property: Property owned just by one spouse. His or her individual property.

Settlor: The legal term for someone who sets up a trust. This person may also be called a grantor, trustor, trust maker, or donor.

Special needs trust: A kind of trust that is established to provide a disabled person with an inheritance without making that person ineligible to receive such government benefits as Supplemental Security Income (SSI) and Medicaid. Also called a supplemental needs trust.

Spendthrift trust: A trust that is set up to benefit someone who is unable to manage his or her own money.

Tangible personal property: Property that you can touch, but not real estate. Examples of tangible personal property include clothing, artwork, vehicles, and jewelry.

Taxable estate: All of the assets in your estate that are subject to federal and state estate taxes.

Tenancy by the entirety: A kind of joint tenancy ownership that some states offer to spouses only.

Tenants in common: A kind of ownership that gives each owner a share of an asset, but not an automatic interest in his or her co-owners' shares when the co-owners die.

Testamentary trust: A trust that is created through your will. Therefore, it does not exist until you die, and it's always irrevocable.

Testator: A person who writes a will.

Trust: A legal entity that is created to hold assets for the benefit of one or more beneficiaries. A trustee manages the trust assets for the benefit of the beneficiary(ies). The maker of the trust is entitled to control what the trust assets and income can be used for and to limit when or if the beneficiaries will receive the assets, among other things. A trust can be a testamentary trust or a living trust.

Trustee: The person who manages the assets in a trust according to the instructions set out in the trust agreement. A bank or trust company may be a trustee.

Uniform Gifts to Minors Act/Uniform Transfers to Minors Act: One or the other version of this law has been adopted by all states. Both laws entitle an adult to set up a custodial account for the benefit of a minor child and to transfer to the account certain types of assets. An adult—a custodian—will manage the assets for the child's benefit, and when the minor becomes a legal adult, he or she gets control over whatever is left in the account. In some states, the adult who sets up the account can require that the child wait until he or she turns 25 to receive the assets.

Will: A legal document used to spell out who will inherit your assets when you die. Also, the parents of minor children designate a personal guardian and a property guardian for those children using a will.

Index

About the Author

John Ventura is a nationally recognized consumer law attorney and author who has been writing about consumer financial and legal issues for more than 18 years. Among other books, he has written *The Will Kit*, 2nd edition, and coauthored *Everything Your Heirs Need to Know*, both of which were published by Kaplan Publishing. He also wrote *Law for Dummies*, 2nd edition, which covers a wide range of legal topics consumers should know about, including estate planning.

John has counseled consumers about estate planning issues during his 30-year legal career, and he has lectured on the subject. Currently he serves as Director of the Texas Consumer Complaint Center at the University of Houston Law School in Texas. He is also an adjunct professor at the law school.

John has been a guest on CNN, CNBC, PBS, and National Public Radio, and he has been quoted in such publications as *The Wall Street Journal, Kiplinger's Personal Finance, Money, Newsweek, Black Enterprise, Entrepreneur, U.S. News & World Report, Maxim, Good Housekeeping, Martha Stewart Living, Chicago Tribune, LA Times, Detroit Free Press, Baltimore Sun, The Indianapolis Star,* and *Dallas Morning News,* among other media outlets. He has also been quoted about consumer issues at CBSMarketWatch.com, Office.com, Bankrate.com, USA Today, MSN Money.com.